PISSED OFF WITH A PURPOSE
WAGING WAR ON FEAR

REMMY STOURAC

Pissed Off with a Purpose

Copyright © Remmy Stourac, 2025.

All rights reserved. No part of this publication may be reproduced, distributed, or transmitted in any form or by any means, including photocopying, recording, or other electronic or mechanical methods, without the prior written permission of the author, except in the case of brief quotations embodied in critical reviews and certain other non-commercial uses permitted by copyright law. For permission requests, contact the author at Remmystourac@hotmail.com

Disclaimer

This book is intended for informational and motivational purposes only. The content reflects the personal experiences and opinions of the author and is not a substitute for professional advice. The author and publisher are not responsible for any diagnosis, treatment decisions, or actions taken based on the material presented in this book. Readers are encouraged to consult appropriate professionals for guidance tailored to their individual circumstances.

The author disclaims any liability for the use, misuse, or interpretation of the content in this book. By reading this book, you acknowledge and agree that the author and publisher are not liable for any potential direct or indirect outcomes resulting from its use.

ISBN

978-1-0693601-0-6 (Paperback)

978-1-0693601-1-3 (Hardcover)

978-1-0693601-2-0 (Ebook)

978-1-0693601-3-7 (Audiobook)

Dedication

To those who know in their bones
That there is more than meets the eye,
That there is a serendipity behind every sorrow,
That there is a worthwhile burden to bear,
That there is bravery in this world.
May you harvest miracles
As you valiantly fumble forward.

Contents

Chapter 1: Not for the Faint of Heart 1
Chapter 2: Gratitude 2.0 12
Chapter 3: Pronoia 28
Chapter 4: Imposter Syndrome 38
Chapter 5: There Are No Dumb Questions 47
Chapter 6: Anthem of a Life 56
Chapter 7: Echoes of Cain 65
Chapter 8: I Could Be a Cowboy… Or Batman! 74
Chapter 9: Humanity 101 95
Chapter 1:0Right Next Door 104
Chapter 11: Let's Talk Freedom 116
Chapter 12: Big Gift Energy 128
Chapter 13: Out of My League? 138
Chapter 14: That Road to Hell 151
Chapter 15: Multi-Dimensionally Jacked 165
Chapter 16: Perfection 180
Chapter 17: Befriend the Monster 189
Chapter 18: A Deranged Future 204
Chapter 19: Stigma 212
Chapter 20: Savage Servitude 224
Chapter 21: The Sharpest Definition 236
Chapter 22: This Mountain is Mine 245
About the Author 252
Thank You + Connect 253
Notes 254

Chapter 1

Not for the Faint of Heart

Pain travels through families until somebody is ready to feel it. For many of us, our generational curse is avoidance. Many of us pretend the injustice of our lives didn't happen and doesn't affect us. Pain demands to be felt. Until somebody in the family dares to feel *everything*, only then can that person shed light on the woes that have unknowingly guided our lives through fear. Yes, this demands that we stumble around in the dark to find ourselves, but we are emboldened in the pursuit.

These people are the generational healers. They transform sorrows into survival guides and can make music of misery. They are all the walking wounded—you and me.

My last book, *An Arsenal of Gratitude,* is like the little brother to this one. It captivated the resilience, hope, and bravery of young cancer survivors through brain tumours, amputations, paralysis, and much more. The courage and audacity I've seen in children with everything against them have proven to me indefinitely that there is bravery in this world.

My life's most profound joys and timeless accomplishments have not been about money or fame. The important victories have unfailingly been around traumas transformed into triumphs. From there, I've used the blooper reel and sincere stack of failure in my life as a stance to laugh and prove there is a worthy fight before us.

I consider my life an experiment. I want to dedicate myself to exceptional habits to acquire exceptional results. I want to take things a little too far to find where the edge truly is. Not missing a gratitude journalling night in seven years builds a perspective I wish I could gift the whole world. This book is an elaborate testimony of my life experiments thus far. Flaws and all.

After getting surgical about gratitude to wage war on my mediocrity and regret, I figured the next ultimate long-term adversary would be my own fear. Let me tell you, years dedicated to waging war on your inadequacy and insecurities brings up an impressive amount of bullshit. But if I don't seek and destroy my bullshit, I keep it, don't I?

I became obsessively curious about emotions. I want to play with them, prod at them, and understand what they are really trying to tell me. Emotions have to be *for* us. Even the awful ones must somehow be pushing us to be healthy, harmonious and fucking magnificent. As my experiments and beliefs have grown, there is no way that emotions are just bad wiring in this absolute miracle of a meat suit that is our body. There is a measure of emotional wizardry and epic action that can transform our sorrows into survival guides. That's what *Pissed Off with a Purpose* is designed to show you.

I may freely speak on some harrowing moments, but I remain a radical optimist. I believe that we are designed not only to survive but also to make monuments, music, art, and love out of what may devastate us. It is the most badass response we can have to tragedy.

If I'm going to lose a childhood friend to cancer, best believe I'm living twice as bold to make the magic of that misery. The love that was there is not lost; it is only transferred over and amplified in his honour. If my friends could grieve that conclusion into existence at the age of twelve, what *can't* we overcome?

My radical optimism is not built on the delusion of pretending bad shit and pure evil isn't real. My optimism is built on the blood, sweat and tears of radical commitment to gratitude, doing the uncomfortable work, and trying to find my personal definition of becoming exceptional. In pursuing and forgiving all the ways I've been an insecure coward, this book is a blanket of evidence for healing and hope.

Here's a secret of many creators that you might not know. Most of us just start creating and have no fucking clue where we are going, but we follow the craft where it intuitively leads us. Only after we figure we are 'done' do we go back to the beginning and try to act like we knew what we were doing all along. That's how I'm rewriting this intro chapter now. But the experiment of overcoming fear, transmuting fear and finding the serendipities after sadness is lifelong. This book is 'the story so far' in my lifelong pursuit to leave this world better than I found it.

I am absolutely terrified to publish this because I speak on profoundly deep things that will meddle with people's self-worth, sense of purpose and freedom in life. But I'm also ever so slightly more compelled to take the chance if it means you can feel the same sincere magnitude of gratitude and enthusiasm for life that I have grown.

I want to drop your jaw with shock and awe. I aspire to translate my mindset and values so that you are left so immeasurably enriched that you can't help but pay the enthusiasm and audacious courage forward. (But also leave reviews… that goes a long way, too!)

In this book, I will be celebrating the aftermaths of amazing friends who've radically transformed their lives after failed suicide attempts, homelessness, psychotic breaks, PTSD, and more. Though it may come across as aggressive and unapologetic, much of my angle stems from operative states of love, grace, gratitude and grit. In what I consider to be the true definition of a friend: Somebody who can have uncomfortable conversations with you in the spirit to stress-test your value and integrity, I hope to come across as that friend. Of course, that ideal friend is also playful, curious, and unapologetic in their expression.

In a visual, *An Arsenal of Gratitude* is like experiencing a smooch on the forehead that sheds all self-sabotage until this moment. It renews your zest and audacity for life with a hearty slap on the ass to get you going. Whereas, *Pissed Off With a Purpose* is like being handed a map to shatter the matrix and a flaming sword to see into the dark before you. You have been assigned a mountain to prove to others that it can be conquered.

The farther you move into the fog and remaster your life experience, all are emboldened and challenged to follow the enthusiasm of their life's calling. Your evolution will embolden a cascade of others along your path. The collective human experience will be enriched by your sincere effort to discover what you are made of. This book holds secrets to boldness that cannot be avoided once heard. You will be haunted by the wisdom of where you have cheated yourself of your wholeness. Finishing this book will kickstart and support radical ownership of your self-mastery.

I understand my power as a writer is that I can summon feelings of discomfort, discontent, guilt, shame, and more. I have no promise that you won't think I sound like an asshole, though I intend for the finale of every chapter to end on an empowering statement to leave you better than I found you. Sometimes, arriving at that point will make one feel quite vulnerable and emotional.

But honestly, if the figurative shoe fits, it means I'm striking a relevant chord. This means that you're in the fight with me to actualize ourselves and shed the sorrows, shame, and inconsistencies we have lived out. I would not expose any feelings if I were not offering faith and proof that massive change and transformation are real and possible for everybody reading. Here, we will celebrate the flaws and frailties that create our human experience. I hope you can laugh, sympathize and feel humbly empowered that our diligence today can be another's deliverance.

I also intend to make your skin crawl just a little bit through appropriate disgust, anger, and sorrow. I'm a storyteller, amigo! This ain't no textbook. This is real life. There are some gut-wrenching moments. But so are there equally miraculous and marvellous joys in this life. Peace and prosperity are far from promised to us. It is an unbelievable privilege to be living in the first generation of worldwide connections and impact. I do not intend to guilt anybody for enjoying all the strange and vast pleasures and experiences we can now find. However, I will heavily press the importance of stress-testing ourselves for hard times so we are not made pathetic and whiny in inconvenience.

We redefine ourselves and our potential with every new experience. Every new friendship. Every conquered inadequacy. In this new age, our attention has been harvested and manipulated to buy into shallow success and fake fulfilment. We have manufactured 'goods' that manufacture human crises as we pursue them. What I believe to be the ultimate failure has come to fruition for many: We are suffering our overabundance. This book offers an arsenal of perspectives and methods to take our magnificence back.

Why I Bet You're Here

You wouldn't touch this book if you weren't interested in conquering fear and injustice, would you? Nah, this book is for those who've felt exquisite pain, misfortune and injustice. Whether it be from the outside world or injustice of our lack of willpower, we all have some form of wound, resentment or bitterness that we wish didn't have so much power over us.

Ladies and gents, we are all already pissed off. Let's do that, just better. Be pissed off with intention. With intelligence. With grace. With your whole soul.

Be mad enough to make a difference; otherwise, your frustration looks like tolerance. And tolerance is how we got here, isn't that so? Ironically, when you manifest all your anger the way it was intended to be, the result is that things are holistically better after you're done.

The mention of accountability will have most people drop this book before completion as if to pretend they didn't hear the calling to rise to the occasion of their own life. This book is for people who want to finally read something with the right frame and actualize their life through adventure and self-discovery. I will advocate endless curiosity, but I will not advocate the toxic loop of self-development that is all study and no actualized courage in the real world. Eventually, you will have and know enough to go fuck around and find out where to start and play in the world. You will have that by the end of this book.

I'll level with you. I'm not a psychologist or any formally educated version of somebody you'd expect to write a book. I am the untraditional guy for the untraditional world unfolding before us. I've qualified myself as a human with fear and an obsession with maximizing the human experience.

Being deeply connected to gratitude is precisely what has equipped me to captivate my fear and anger for the ways of the world and be intimately entangled with the worst-case scenario. In a valiant effort against those worst cases, I build a life and become somebody who can survive and thrive despite all the misery that may come my way. This art of gratitude is to become anti-fragile and sincerely cherish the goodness in our life before it passes.

The most bitter people are also some of the laziest. They consider themselves victims of the world and have positioned themselves as powerless. Despite us all being powerful individuals, some have nothing but complaints to offer while other people go and make the difference they want to see in the world. If you are afraid to look at your own soul, then this book is not for you.

If you're pissed off at the world for not kneeling at your convenience, then this book will offend you. With intention, I must add. I have to call out the ways that we experience anger that makes us weak if I'm going to be able to walk you through transmuting that rage into something divine. If you're *divinely* pissed off, this book will amplify the peace you have. We might even feel like family in arms after this crazy ride.

A Kindergarten teacher friend told me how she helped the 5-year-olds understand their emotions as if they were a snow globe. If you're all flustered, the sparkles fly all over, and it's hard to see clearly through the sparkle storm. So, if you feel called out or provoked by any of this content, please consider letting your sparkles settle before you continue or act rashly.

There is no virtue in being harmless. If we are to appreciate and embrace goodness, we might as well use that time as an opportunity to defend ourselves and goodness as a whole. Otherwise, the wicked and selfish only have to patiently creep in as we become pathetic and defenceless from abusing our privilege of safety and security.

I am a massive advocate of grace, compassion, and forgiveness. But people who capitalize on the virtues of others need a more straightforward and ruthless remedy. Standards with grace will be your best friend for prosperous and harmonious relationships. Even good and gentle people require a stiff spine. If you cannot defend yourself and instill your harmonious justice, then your mercy has no value.

Your ability to discern who deserves your selflessness develops your value. If you cannot say no, then you, too, are somebody whose energy will be thanklessly harvested. There is a big difference between being valuable and being valued.

We are also going to have fun, though. Nobody likes being purely serious. The ultimate conclusion is not a life of serious achievement but a childlike playfulness and zest for possibility on this strange ride. Achievement is terrific, but if you were popping blood vessels in your eyes to justify your existence, that's a hard sell for the next generation. But if we have a future where we can grow as badass, courageous individuals who never lose playfulness for the absurdity and depth of human discovery, the future will remain in good hands.

Being a grumpy, resentful worry-warrior is a lame ass way to live. I'll put it plainly: Your emotions are indicators, not dictators.

If you feel a lack of harmony or powerlessness, the adventure of your empowerment is right there screaming at you. Where your fear, resentment, or discomfort is, there is your task. We are in the age of endless information. But becoming 'wise' and remaining a coward will only multiply your bitterness. That's why supposed 'smart' people grow bitter at 'dumb' people for having more courage than them simply because they spent less time hesitating. Those with a healthy sense of courage will celebrate all other's courageousness in this life. Only in one's own reflection of cowardice would one look at another's valiant efforts and wish to stifle the expansion of another human being.

To be 'exceptional' is to be the exception. To be misunderstood. To be outside the norm. Wave-makers are aliens to those swept away in the societal tide bestowed upon them. You are either being influenced or being influential. The human spirit is born free. We are born playful and without remorse for crying and expressing our needs. We must return to who we were before the world's temptations got their hands on us. We must know who we are and what gifts we have to offer to genuinely 'play' with humanity in a fruitful way.

Are you a resentful passenger on a boat you didn't ask to be sailing on? Or are you the master of your sails?

We Are Enough

Knowledge is not power; only applied knowledge is power. Although I wish to entertain, I desire even more deeply that you feel your intuition loud and clear. Your self-actualization and enthusiasm for life are the ultimate gifts you offer yourself and all others.

If we *become* more, we have more to offer. We don't owe anybody anything, but being a willing participant in the well-being of others is to wage war on misery itself. What more noble task might there be? There is no passive way through this life. We are either normalizing a pursuit of human potential or normalizing the shortcoming of it.

Sure, you have a job, some hobbies and possibly a family to care for. Then what? Eat, sleep, work, poop, and casually unwind as an audience member to the world unfolding? The governments are unhinged and inching towards taking our rights little by little. AI is evolving and shifting society faster than most can prepare for. We have enough nukes to all be liquefied in minutes if somebody was fed up enough. And we are just… waiting it out? How are you truly living with this incredibly terrifying and miraculous jaunt through life?

I'm pissed off that we fear pathetic things. Like saying hello. Like asking questions. Asking for help. Asking for patience. Asking for clarity. Asking for space. Asking for boundaries and the bare minimum of respect when people project their misplaced frustration on others.

We fear sitting in the silence of our own thoughts. We fear walking into businesses we aren't familiar with. We fear *ideas* that challenge our own and call them 'others' and 'enemies.' If we could only call these things out for how ridiculous they are, it could conjure the bare minimum courage to overcome constant anxiety.

We are fearfully and wonderfully made. If I can only convince you what an absolute force of nature you can be, the world will thank you for your contribution. I want you to be intelligent and dangerous. Selfish people who tend to thrive on the insecurities or innocence of others have no idea how to handle somebody with healthy self-respect. It can be and is that simple.

Did you know there isn't anything about you that wasn't made for your own good? Desire to us is wants and wishes. But the Latin origin, *'de sidere'* literally translates to "from the stars" or "from a heavenly body." Now I realize that's why we want the 'stars to align.' Because both our earthly body and the heavenly body desire unity. For my desires and the desires of creation itself to be in harmony. You don't have to be spiritual for that to be badass.

But riddle me this: How has this divine intelligence been so corrupted to bring us this far into the future but now tear us apart from within? It's the same tool. The same weapon. The intelligence that no two people will have quite the same. So uniquely so that it makes each one of us irreplaceable in value. Even with that blatantly apparent, we treat each other with savage impatience and disregard.

We are weird, unique, lost, and imperfect. Yet, we are made new every day. We insanely undervalue our own potential. Insecurity literally translates as underestimating ourselves.

Most of all... I think we are pissed off that our desires have been lead astray. This intelligence 'from the stars' has been made small instead of infinite. We have been left feeling aimless instead of masters of our fate. It made us feel like we can't make a change because we are so married to our comforts that our primal hunger has beaten our intuition and free will into submission. These earthly desires that do not align with our interconnected potential are precisely why we feel disconnected and alone in the most interwoven era the world has ever known.

The divine wisdom of injustice that brews from our anger has been manipulated in pathetic and insecure ways. With this corrupted and fearful manifestation, we leave things in ruin rather than renew the goodness it was intended for. Our madness is such an untapped, misunderstood magnificence to behold. It's the heart of every underdog, every revolution, every upgrade in humanity that vibrates in our souls that there is bravery in this world.

We need to bring the divinity back to our fear and anger. So, its subtleties leave memories of, 'Something is about to get better' instead of 'Dad's home, stay out of his way.'

We have a long way to go, friends. But I'm giving this everything I got. Thankfully, we are designed for mastery that grows with every new day. There is plenty of hope that our future generations will transcend from our efforts in the glory the stars intended for us.

I am plenty human. Chalked full of flaws and fears enough to fill a yacht. But I concluded in my first life message in *An Arsenal of Gratitude* that our full actualization is not a transcendence but a homecoming to what potential was intended for us all along. Falling short of that is worth being pissed off about. Rewiring our sense of injustice from only ourselves to the harmonious whole of humanity is where we take our magnificence back. This is the rising tide that raises all ships.

This, my friends, is being pissed off with a purpose.

Chapter 2

Gratitude 2.0

Gratitude is the definition of what sustains your striving.
If somebody could gift you 10,000 moments of your own life worth being grateful for, do you not think that would be the ultimate tribute to the goodness around you? I've written those 10,000 noteworthy moments of life in the last seven years. This discipline comes with a unique set of insights into the human experience.

I'm starting with gratitude in *Pissed Off with a Purpose* because of three reasons:

1. It builds a conscious connection of my role in my life and how the world and people respond to my part in this weird journey. There is no shortage of surprises and mystery around every corner. When you sow the best of yourself into existence, you're allowed to gratify that. The world can't help but respond in profound and unexpected ways. Building this journal of evidence that goodness is alive and working in the world allows you to feel the unfathomable interconnectedness of it all.

2. Gratitude helps me not sweep any sad, embarrassing, angry, regretful or shameful experiences under the rug, allowing me a profound sense of power. It allows me to become anti-fragile and profit spiritually, emotionally and mentally from all my struggles. When I speak to my soul every night about

whether I am proud of who I am today, I keep a constant dialogue with my ambitions. I consult my younger *and* older self to see whether I've honoured my sense of self-actualization and what that demands. Becoming more of *me* is the gift I offer others in this life.

3. Taking a profound account of life's hardships allows me to know where I'm responsible and where I am simply at the mercy of human hardship. There is true power in taking ownership of where *I* am the problem. It means I can change. If I cannot change the world or others, I am challenged to align my spirit as a victor or victim of circumstance. Who I choose to be after devastation or heartbreak is where I prove the mettle of my human spirit. There are unspeakable horrors and pain to experience in this life. But living with a zest that life is still worth living allows all others the proof that the human spirit is genuinely indomitable.

Gratitude journaling creates an opportunity to double-dip on life's goodness. It even lets you triple-dip when you teach others how to actualize their appreciation for life. When you sit back every night and ask yourself, "What mattered today?" Your answers will always be filtered through what provoked the most emotion out of you. You can try to reflect chronologically, but you'll know by the order of importance in which your mind presents the answer to that question.

Our first universal language is emotion. Then, language becomes secondary to transmuting that with others. That's why we fail to communicate our desires, feelings and intent. If we can get in tune and become emotionally literate, we also amplify our connection to others.

I write this after a close friend surprised me with a photo of their journal from five months prior. She quoted some uplifting words I shared to ease her mind as she navigated a new life after calling off her marriage. I reciprocated with my journal entry about how proud

I was of her when she shared that she visited her parents, put on her wedding dress, and danced with her dad despite things not falling together as expected. In light of her worries, her most significant focus was hoping her ex was finding the strength to move forward, too. In a moment where she could have taken on a woe-is-me mentality, her heart still wished her ex a life of bliss and beauty.

Five months later, we laugh at how overbearing those stresses were in the moment. Yet, this could be considered the distant past now for how little those experiences weigh on our current moment. New people have entered and left. New hopes and dreams came into focus. Every day has a unique way of surprising us. Dare I say I even found the quadruple-dip moment with what happened next!

I shared a video with this friend of a man who asks random homeless people for a favour when they have barely anything to give. If they were able to perform any minuscule kindness, like splitting a donut or giving away one of their cans of soup, he would surprise them with $1000.

"What a dream this lifestyle would be!" I shared to her. I realized I had just journaled the day she sent me $100 for five of my *Arsenal of Gratitude* books she gave to her friends. She went out of her way to help me feel it was a gift worth sharing.

I told her she was the equivalent of that man to me in moments like that. This visceral appreciation seems beyond words to say thank you when somebody celebrates my work and takes it upon themselves to share it, too. She took absolutely zero gain from helping me and even refused my offer to split the profit, considering it would not exist otherwise. She still refuses, so I hope this noteworthy appreciation reciprocates the kindness here. You are the kind of friend people pray for, Alyssa. It is a great pleasure to immortalize a thank-you for friends like you in this book.

The first double-dip was teaching her the value of gratitude journaling. The triple-dip slapped back when she occasionally sends appreciation moments when she gets to reminisce on times that I impacted her day and remind me, in turn, that my presence was valued. The fourth layer of goodness was that timely moment to share that heartwarming video and parallel a memory where she may not be able to bless people financially to such a grandiose degree. Still, her character does the job just the same. If there is one easy promise, you will grow tired of being written into somebody's history as a moment worth remembering.

A gratitude journal is a mental and emotional photo album that only you can see. Your spirit still has snapshots of the emotion stored in your being, and you can revisit that richness as often as you like. It is a form of emotional wealth available to all, but few ever capitalize on it.

Speaking To My Own Soul

A gratitude chapter is first up in this book because if you don't have the diligence to take 3-5 minutes daily to account for your blessings, how can I trust you to handle the harsher stuff? Gratitude is literally the positive emotional handout that you can give *yourself*. And to others, for that matter. Before you proceed, please stop and count five things you're grateful for. And Go!

Hell yes! Look at you go. I'm assuming positive intent because that's how you build rapport. *Winky face.*

When people ask, 'How do you know what to journal about?' I was baffled by how to simplify that for a long time. But as you wing what you assume to be valuable, you subconsciously narrate your own values to yourself by what you decide to write down about your day. As I have exposed to myself that one of my top two fears is deteriorating memory, the most significant question I can ask myself now is, 'What is worth remembering?'

That is a loaded question. What about the things we would rather forget? By asking that, you might think, if I choose not to journal some things, perhaps I will forget!

Oh, we wish that were the case, don't we? The more critical question revealed was, 'What am I going to do about the things I would rather forget but know that I can't?'

I am positive that just about everybody has some skeletons in their closet. We harbour guilt, shame, insecurities, and shortcomings that we would prefer not to showcase to the world. I am no different. We are the only people who spend every waking moment with ourselves. That means I need to have conversations with myself that nobody else can have. We tend to consider that if nobody knows, maybe we can mentally sweep some of our memories under the rug and pretend some parts of our story never happened. It is a seemingly harmless ideal. But this has drastic long-term effects. A gratitude journal will expose that in due time.

I learned that translating thoughts onto a physical page or even notes on a device creates a roadmap to defeat over-thinking. When we write down a string of thoughts and what we know (to the best of our limited perspective) of how things are, we create a physical manifesto of our internal experience.

If I died and left behind a journal of all my worries and anxieties that people may disregard in communication, they would have no choice but to admit they were genuine if they read it in that journal, right? It created a space to actualize and organize the things that the outside world can convince me I'm crazy for feeling. There is nothing crazy about suffering, worry, or confusion. It's the same that nothing is crazy about our joy, clarity, or convictions. It's all our personal story. Fleeting moments will pass whether we like it or not.

If we don't humanize our experience for ourselves and validate our emotions and experiences, we can't rewrite a narrative we refuse to admit affected us. As I previously said, abnormal reactions to abnormal situations are normal behaviour. If something strange, new, or unexpected happens, we cannot expect ourselves to know our reaction to things we've never experienced. Of course, this is where we insert grace, compassion and patience, but we suck at that, too, when things get unhinged.

All this considered, my journaling is lighthearted and joyful, as much as it can sometimes be gruelling and uncomfortable. It is deeply personal. If you're honestly staring yourself in the soul when you try to reflect on each of your days, you will have conversations that nobody but you can have with yourself. When you're being honest and doing the emotional math of where you spend your time, you can gauge how truly holistically disciplined and content you are. What you reveal after this is how willing you are to change the trajectory of your life when you are not satisfied with what makes up your day.

There are certainly self-conversations I intend to share that make up the backbone of this book. They are hard-earned after years of reflecting, and it may just fast-forward years of battling our bullshit. Even if I share my personal story, simply relating can feel abrasive and like I'm calling you out. If you think that, that means it is precisely the sort of substance that will grow you. Don't touch a book about waging war on fear if you want to stay comfortable. The training wheels are taken off for this kind of growth.

We all sell each other our highlight reels at introductions. People are desperate to pretend they have it all together because we know how uncontrollable and chaotic we are behind the scenes.

Only we fall asleep with ourselves every night and barter over the value of our souls. Many conversations, seasons, and 4:00 AM nights lead to creating a version of myself that respects himself. A quote that stuns me every time and reminds me how far I've come in twenty-seven years is, *"Nobody will ever know the violence that it took to become this gentle."*

It is *not* necessary to welcome people into every season that created you. Whatever you are willing to share is a very intimate thing that I hope you treat delicately. This way, you present it to people who can adequately celebrate the magnitude of what you're working towards and what you've overcome thus far. I will never be able to accurately present a long-gone version of myself to the new people I find in life. But, the quality of people that become my new circle as I grow older will accurately depict who I am becoming. Those who we find home in along the way are significant indicators of whether we surround ourselves with people who want and demand our evolution or co-sign our bullshit to stay stagnant, stuck and powerless.

Gratitude doesn't mean everything is beautiful and without stress. Here are a few notes that show gratitude in humility. Every exposure to a shortcoming is an opportunity to grow.

#1044. On receiving my first round of editor's feedback for *An Arsenal of Gratitude*: 7207 revisions for me to review. I appreciate Ogden's genuine effort and can't wait for all I might learn from this.

#1770. Cold sweats driving home, narrowly avoided shitting my pants. (This moment inspired a written portion in the chapter 'Right Next Door.')

#5214. Joining my first Alcoholics Anonymous session to support a friend and hearing other's reflections and humility ended up adding value against my self-depreciating ways.

Bursting My Tiny Bubble

I don't think we all grasp how unfathomable our minds are. It is so obsessed with its wiring of reality that we often forget our power to change it. We envelop ourselves in our world and its problems and can only attack it from our limited understanding.

For example, I confided in my friend Jeremy about my dilemma of whether to invest my only $5,000 into getting *An Arsenal of Gratitude* published or replace the old faithful first truck that suddenly got the death wobble on me. As I bounced back the pros and cons of my decisions, Jeremy looked me dead in the face and said, "You understand you have *good* problems, right?"

"What do you mean?" I asked, already realizing this was about to recalibrate my soul.

"You're telling me the *biggest* issue right now is publishing a book or reluctantly having to say goodbye to your first vehicle? Some people *wish* they had your problems. You're sitting on an incredible opportunity or possibly waiting a little longer if replacing Li'l Blue (the truck) is necessary. This isn't a real problem. It's an inconvenience."

My dilemma went from a 'problem' to realizing, 'Oh wow! I've orientated my life to such a place that the worst thing I could comprehend at *that* moment was to move my creative career forward or find a new freedom wagon.' For a guy publishing a book on gratitude, my friend thoroughly humbled me. I went from thinking I had a problem to relaxing and remembering that I was healthy and on course for a legacy-level life project by the age of 23. The possibility that a friend will drop into your life and have the proper conversation at the right time to shift the paradigm of your thinking could happen any day. This chance multiplies with the number of meaningful connections and the quality of the people in your circle.

To emphasize how sentimental this truck was, it kept my older brother and me alive through some dangerous predicaments. Half were self-inflicted. But the appropriate send-off felt like limping it back 100 miles to the family farm to load it with Tannerite and blast the angels free for all the hell it got us through. Goodbyes are not always so seamless as the truck was auctioned off for parts. In retrospect, it was simply a truck that did us well, but in spirit, it deserved a redneck sendoff to vehicular Valhalla.

I've been obsessed with 'good problems' ever since. The difference is that a dumb problem is something reoccurring and avoidable. Experiencing a dumb problem for the first time deserves our grace because we didn't know. It couldn't be a dumb problem if we were genuinely ignorant. A problem that reoccurs by avoiding or neglecting a conversation, maintenance or fear of confrontation is a dumb problem. You either face it once, and the situation evolves or resolves. Not facing it and allowing it to stay is how you practice powerlessness.

Also, a dumb problem can be caused by exaggerating a minor issue into something major. You are only as stable as the most minor thing that will trigger you. People can weaponize this emotional instability against you. Nobody can save you from your lack of self-maintenance. You are either amplifying the harmony in a situation or playing a role in the discourse—victim or otherwise.

A 'good' problem, on the other hand, could be an opportunistic dilemma. A 'good' problem is knowing your needs are all met and that the decision you're faced with is that of abundance and excess. A 'good' problem is getting to argue with somebody you love rather than having nobody to love at all. A 'good' problem is facing growing pains on your terms rather than being forced through hardship. A 'good' problem is having choices to make rather than having no choice at all. A 'good' problem is what freedom feels like. Like Having more opportunities and choices than we know how to manage well. Lastly, A 'good' problem is ANY inconvenience. Inconvenience is an opportunity to hone your self-regulation. Alternatively, assuming the privilege that the world should be easy for you is a dumb problem. That is the active mindset of believing the world is against you.

Gratitude note #2088: Marcus taught me, during a bout of disheartenment, 'God doesn't give you exactly as much as you can handle. He gives you *more* than you can handle, so you can learn to lean on faith for the rest.'

Journaling will become a grossly exposing indicator of where we spend our time. Journaling is not just writing down your day. It is bargaining with how content you are about showing up for your own life. It is not for the faint of heart. That is why we are fearfully and wonderfully made. To do complicated things and prosper through discomfort at every waking moment. As hard as we try to write our lives from an unbiased space, barely a few weeks or months pass before we look back and laugh at how far we've come.

You'll see how minor your problems were in those days. Without realizing it, the 'worst' things at any given moment will be short-lived and even soon forgotten. Then we arrive at true tragedy and forget that we were amid 'the good ole days' all along. What a tragedy to miss that.

You will never *not* have problems. New problems are the spice of life. In contrast, repetitive problems breed discouragement and depression.

On the brighter side, you become a rarity of somebody with a road map of the consequences of your life. Reading a book on relationship conflict resolution instead of binge-watching TV becomes how you can thank your past self for investing in the skills that make you an emotional wizard in de-escalating arguments that used to be huge fights. Thanking yourself for the time you invest in yourself creates the validation that you are preparing yourself for the arena of life. You get to craft your swagger when you know damn well you've built yourself to be somebody that others breathe easier around. That is no small task, and your future will pay back epic dividends in the quality of your relationships due to those self-investments.

To be brutally honest, I don't skip to my room and love the idea of journaling each night. In fact, my friends have witnessed if I've stayed over and am nearing passing out when I suddenly mutter, 'Son-of-a-bitch... I have to journal.' Then I grab my phone and am curled over in my bed or on a friend's couch with one eye open in deep exhaustion as I hold myself accountable. Doing things your future self will be proud of isn't comfortable. However, creating it as a non-negotiable builds the first element of consistency that you can build the rest of your life around.

Nevertheless, onwards! To show how gratitude and being pissed off with a purpose are two peas in a pod.

Why People Are Afraid to Be Grateful

Through this four-year journey studying fear, I've discovered that the opposite of fear is love. For those people who pawn off gratitude as fluffy or lame, I pose this to you: I bet you feel that way about gratitude because you're terrified to take an inventory of your life. Because then you'd have to realize that you aren't showing up to your full capacity. Or you are willingly avoiding fighting for things that matter to you to your full capability. Here is an example.

I met an amazing new friend in the recovery community thanks to Instagram. We hopped on a video call and got right to celebrating our darkest days as the place where we build our humility and future. This friend (a complete stranger at the time) admitted one of the most amazing things to me when they began their gratitude journey. He wanted to make a list of things worth fighting for as both he and his wife were trying to get sober from heroin for the sake of their young child after it cost him 9 months in prison. It was his parents who said to him and his wife, "It's a miracle our grandchild has been so healthy and happy despite your addictions tearing everything else apart."

That sobering sentence made this man realize the *only* thing he was grateful for could be his family. Every other thing took a backseat or was leveraged to get more heroin at that time. The potency of gratitude is an instilled power that says, 'I will fight for you.' That's why no other thing could make the gratitude list besides family. Everything else was sold, pawned, or traded to keep the habit that would kill them if they didn't soon conquer it.

That's why gratitude is not fluffy. It's a word we use to wage war against sorrow and suffering. It tells you where you really show up for life. If you lie to yourself about your effort, your regret will surely fill the void where your gratitude was not the driving force.

It was the appropriate fury in that man's sense of injustice that allowed him to realize the only thing keeping him alive was his family. His selfishness was the injustice that was keeping his family barely alive. Gratitude made him stare his brokenness in the face. Gratitude was the life-saving practice that exposed his wounds that he wasn't mending, therefore making him bleed on those who didn't cut him. He would have to look his family in the eye and say he wasn't grateful enough to recover for them.

But he was made of stronger stuff. He let gratitude guide the way in every recovery step for himself *and* his wife. Now, they have made themselves living survival guides to aid others in their recovery from substance abuse.

So, I'm pissed off that people casually belittle gratitude as if it's not the highest virtue on the totem pole. Gratitude is for those who aren't afraid to take an inventory of their own life. Gratitude is for the brave who can see the significant cost of doing the right thing and be willing to pay the price, even if it's not promised to work out. Gratitude builds the internal compass that takes the entire world and shows you everything at your disposal to make moves that matter to you. If you took an inventory of all the blessings right before you, you'd have to admit you're the only thing in your way. You won't see it all at once, but it's a mental muscle that strengthens as you use it.

You would astound yourself if you dared look at everything within your power. You wouldn't want to search for that only because you'd have to admit you've been selling yourself short all along. It's a small price of humility to pay not to perpetuate the bullshit you've sold yourself that keeps you unsatisfied with your own life.

If there is a hierarchy of reactions to everything in life, I can dumb it down to this: Finding a way to be grateful for a new lesson and exploring ways you were built to triumph over this latest tragedy is the most divine response. It is not immediate but imminent. As for bitching and moaning, it's somewhere beneath that. Choose wisely.

Foreboding Joy

You might ask, "Well, dang, Remmy. What about the things that seem to end too soon despite our best efforts?"

Thousands of notes of gratitude later, you get some clarity that things only suck in proportion to how wonderful it was. Just because something ended does not mean it was wrong. We are so terrified of endings that we become terrified of the hard work and conversations that can lead to a deepening quality. We are afraid the conversation or effort of strengthening a good thing is worse than never letting something reach its full potential. How silly is that? We have this obsession of 'forever' that comes in fairy tales, and we lose grip on loving something or somebody while it is right here in front of us.

The term 'Foreboding Joy' refers to when the experience of joy is interrupted by the thought of 'What if something bad happens?' Many of us are so used to good things inevitably ending that if we see no external threat, we worry that *we* are the bad thing that could happen.

We brood on our inadequacy and our fears of unworthiness as 'the bad thing that could happen.' We make decisions on others' behalf and self-sabotage our joy and its growth in sheer terror of the mere thought that this good thing will hurt when it ends. So, we defy that fear by being radically authentic. We surrender our true selves to those who will genuinely love and accept our raw selves—not just the caricature we offer to hope we receive affection in return.

We grieve in direct proportion to how much something mattered to us. That grief will either be in gratitude for how lucky we were while it lasted OR in the sorrow of stifled happiness while we had the chance.

The fact that things end is why there is pressure on value in the first place. 'Forever' has done more harm than any other promise ever made. Forever is the enemy of gratitude. It belittles the preciousness of our limited time here together. 'Forever' softens our sense of discipline and creates a falsehood bound to shatter the sweetness of holding onto something that can disappear at any moment. 'Forever' fractures our freedom and diminishes our choices to love diligently. 'Forever' creates assumptions and expectations that cannot be sustained through the flexibility that life will demand of ever-changing seasons and needs.

I don't want to end this on a bummer note. On the contrary, I've been continually forced (through my own design) to experience my goodbyes twice in how I practice gratitude. I delay my digital to physical journaling by 3-5 months. I relive all my appreciation well after it has passed.

There is a bittersweetness to revisiting every standout moment across an entire relationship, *knowing* I will also have to revisit the intricate details. Heartbreak and highlights alike. However, knowing that I hold myself accountable every night, I am inclined to invest my entire being into something I will choose to revisit. It's a reminder that if I shied out from what mattered, I can note the moment I let fear win. The journal will portray a gradual decline that I may have genuinely had power over if I wasn't such a coward.

And I have been that coward.

It eats at the very core of our being. That price of moving towards fear with somebody you love is so astoundingly less painful than the aftermath of validating self-inflicted fears and watching them come to life. You will be left to slow dance with the ghosts of what could have been when you *know* you left things unsaid and undone while you had the chance.

The twenty promises I published at the end of *An Arsenal of Gratitude* paved my way to winning that war against my fears. There is now a unique sweetness to revisiting those 3-5 months of delayed physical journaling. I can reminisce fondly about the people and moments I have met so profoundly.

The mundane ceases to exist when your guiding force becomes a spiritual hunter of beauty and opportunity. I could have been anywhere else, doing anything else, but I was there. Doing that. It's all I had, and I didn't miss out on how special that was.

The greatest flex that my gratitude practice has created is that I can stare people I know and love in the face and say without a shadow of a doubt, "I don't miss a fucking beat of how significant your presence is in my life." I have living proof written by hand in case they have a moment of doubt and need to see every reminder I have for them. It's not perfect, but the messiness is the flavour of how my best grapples with others and draws such incredible things out of what has broken me before.

So, I implore you to take inventory of your life and use every tool in your arsenal to fight for it. If you think gratitude is still fluffy, you'll come back to this exact practice when you're cleaning up the aftermath of losing touch with your blessings. The quality of your present moment stands entirely on this practice.

Here is a note to myself written on Jan 10, 2021, after the first 1896 notes and filling my first leather journal to the brim.

Dear Remmy,

You incredibly capable mofo.

You began when your heart was broken, and your soul was sick. Look what miracles have been hiding in 1.6 years. Your heart is massive... and growing.

You barely skimmed the surface of how good it is going to get. Life has such incredible plans for you.

Keep your head up. You make magic out of madness. You prosper in pain. You aren't perfect, but man, you will shake the world.

God bless. We are going to win this thing.

Signed, Remmy Stourac

I dare you to fill one journal to the absolute brim with memories and leave a note to your younger self. Create a moment in which you constantly converse with your future self. This note is paying dividends on my serenity three years later and still counting. I hope you get mad enough to count your blessings.

CHAPTER 3

Pronoia

Have you ever tried the opposite of paranoia? Pronoia is the conscious practice of pondering things working out better than the ideal—not only simply things going well, but even better than well. This practice smashed my entire paradigm and inspired me to drop my current reality and take a thirty-two-hour road trip to the great white Canadian north to trial a helicopter piloting career.

I will offer you this rule for life that changed the entire landscape of how I play with life. I was three years into building this book before having the gall to establish this for myself. So, prepare for this meditation and practice to bring up some significant feelings. Before you play with the ways of the world, you must manage the ways of your own nature. If you have a habit of stifling your enthusiasm and curiosity about your desires, then you have little merit to lead or influence others' courage.

This is a book about maximal walking to prove our talk. The less you can theorize and the more you can live, the more captivated you can be and remain in genuine flow with life, love, and opportunity.

This new rule set out the ultimate adventure of my year. It is simply this:

I can no longer reject myself. Other people, society, or the world have to reject me first.

Once you ask yourself and make an honest list of how you have gotten in your own way, you may feel shame, anger, sorrow, or other emotions. But let there also be some proud feelings that you took the first step to shed light on some of our most defeating blind spots. We can be so committed to our internal narrative of why we didn't act. Whether on an opportunity, asking out a person, or letting days, weeks, and years go by, avoiding what we say we've wanted all along. Perhaps the list could be long, but after 3-5 things, you already have enough ideas to challenge your beliefs. Start conquering one instance at a time rather than ponder a lifelong list of shortcomings. It can be a slippery slope of self-depreciating thoughts against the spirit of this practice.

When trailing horses through the Northwest Territories as a Big Game Horseback Hunting Guide with my two older brothers, I was also exposed to the lifestyle of bush pilots. There is a power, freedom, and fantasy of being the first era of humanity to fly over this vast creation with which we have been given to play. My life is already strange enough, so I humoured the thought of becoming a pilot and had that fantasy shot down when Google told me aspiring pilots could not have any heart conditions. Having had three heart procedures and experiencing some significant heart palpitations, it just sounded like 'Duh. Don't let the guy with a fluttery heart become Mr. Dangerous-Transportation.'

Initially, I was grateful for that clarity so I couldn't have an excitable side track when perhaps I was getting imposter syndrome about being a philanthropic author. I dialled in and kept writing. But this rule leads me back to smite my bullshit. I've been living with the mindset that despite my best efforts for health and fitness, I have a 'limiting' heart condition. With this new rule, if I was doing my proper due diligence and walking my talk, I had to get that mindset medically confirmed.

The following day, I called an Aviation Medical Examiner. Fast-forward a week of x-rays, heart readings, and various sensory tests, and I passed with flying colours! The examiner heard my initial concerns and said, "You're not an old chubby guy who gave himself diabetes from neglect. You're a young, healthy man, and it's crazy if you *don't* go for it."

I lived with a decade of believing that specific careers were outside my destiny because of that limiting belief. There is some serious glamour in the perception of helicopter pilots, the lifestyle, the possibility, etc. So not only did my glass ceiling break, but a sexy, admirable new career could be within reach. I started looking up schools and faced the $80,000 (minimum) school and licence costs. There was now so much momentum and excitement for a sudden life trajectory change because of this *one* new rule to not reject myself.

But the plot thickens.

A lot.

Serendipities

So, I consider the one and only heli-pilot contact I had nine years previously from horseback guiding. My first impression of the Yukon was being welcomed into this man's house for my first-ever lobster dinner. My family was dined to the max before living off the grid for nearly four months. Generous on his part towards my whole family was an understatement.

I called him up and reintroduced myself, saying I'd appreciate any time he could spare to prepare me for a pilot career. I had already applied and put down a deposit for a school starting in September and was prepared to bite the $80,000 bullet for this life shift.

Fifteen minutes into a phone call with this man, he asks, "Why don't you come to work for me as ground crew and find out for yourself?"

Besides, "Absolutely!" I asked a few logistical questions and suddenly had fifty days to uproot my life. I couldn't feel luckier to have a leg up in a competitive and limited industry, let alone a promised position afterward. I was even warned by the school instructor that 'These old pilot boys don't like zoom calls. So, if you aren't willing to drive across the country and knock on doors to make an impression, don't bother getting a licence.'

Most of the stress that could come with this was all falling to the wayside, and it felt like destiny. I merely had to smite my bullshit. I was in absolute shock that so much of an opportunity was being laid before me after I got out of my own way. As well as how willing the universe was willing to conspire in my favour from a few good first impressions across a decade.

Ironically, a major part of my willingness to uproot was not having a romantic partner to consider with the distance. Within a week of this unfolding, an old flame was reignited the day before my birthday. With only three weeks before I left, it was unreasonable to consider a long-term relationship unfolding. But celebrating a grand new beginning until the end was a bittersweetness worth feeling.

Despite logic (as love does), a fantastic momentum couldn't help her saying, "Fuck this. You're worth waiting for!"

Oh, how the strands of life twist and turn.

Despite the sorrow, the shock and awe of the unknown before me had me buzzing excitedly. I was living the example of my courageous new law and receiving an unfathomable new beginning in a village of 400 with no cell service within 100km. I was fortunate to have shoddy Wi-Fi to send a text that sometimes took half a day to send. On this helicopter outfit in Atlin, BC, a camper trailer would be my home for the next two months.

The lifestyle of those living truly in the freedom of the great North had unlimited potential. Community was genuinely thick, as all you really had out there was each other. Grocery runs were a whole-day fiasco, as driving two hours to Whitehorse, Yukon, was more realistic than triply expensive necessities in this little village.

I got to learn and support the efforts of geologists pulling rocks and geodes off the mountains. We pulled thousands of pounds of salmon from the fisheries. We slung vital gear out to the mining operations. We did tours of one of the most enormous glaciers left in North America. We brought firefighters out after storms to check where lightning struck to ensure no forest fires were starting. It felt like I was an integral part of the wild north's evolution and way of life.

And the people! My god, the people are so genuine, rowdy and unique. You had to be a pretty wild specimen to endure the unforgiving conditions of the freezing north, but it came with a character and resilience that embraced every ray of sunshine in its rare warmth of short summers. Every person I crossed had so much pep in their step and a rich history to be proud of. Some were paving their way from across the world to plant their own roots. Others were native families, establishing harmony with the north and preserving its wild ways.

With all this richness in each day and even a loving woman back home to relay the beauty of it all as the elusive Wi-Fi permitted, it felt like a nonstop dream. There was no shortage of serious labour and long days with 23 hours of sunlight in the summer. It was a wholly new life.

I was reflecting on my values and wondered how truly aligned they were with my ultimate design. As I discovered more details of the reality before me and my commitment to this new life, I had to take a hard inventory of the actual price of this.

With a million-and-one positive things to say about this, following this path would, in some sense, cost me my dream of becoming a philanthropic author. My bones and spirit are deeply attuned to leaving people and places better than I found them, and this remote wonderland would cost me eight months of solitude a year. Even my boss said in our original phone call, "It's a good thing you're single because this career is *really* hard on relationships."

Shit, man, rough selling point.

I had to take an inventory of my true gifts compared to my skill sets. My true gift is communicating, inspiring, encouraging and shattering people's limitations. In contrast, my skill set is to learn to work harder than anybody else and be of ultimate value despite the dollar figure I'm getting paid. I'm a construction company's dream labourer. But at the end of the day, I'm significantly more concerned with spiritual, mental, emotional and relational richness than monetary. The pilot glamour, the sexy reputation, the adventure and all is more than anybody could ask for. I pondered whether this was another stint of subtle cowardice to embrace the cost ahead of me or whether I realized this was not in ultimate alignment with my fulfilment.

I also note how fortunate I am to be somebody who can consider his freedom and happiness. Many people are skimming by, and I was just above safe enough to risk it all. Radical gratitude allowed me to feel so abundant with so little that I was leaving nothing behind in my original home in Kelowna other than friendships and a lucky rental situation. At the end of the day, I desire to play with the unlimited potential and be more deeply interwoven in people's stories through my volunteering, social impact and following my enthusiasm.

This is an appropriate moment to say that the origin of the word 'enthusiasm' is to be inspired or possessed by God's energy. There is an intuition that, if listened to, cannot always be explained. It can only be followed and lived. It is not promised to unfold seamlessly, but it will be a story-worthy and evolutionary choice in our experience.

I also felt it was dishonourable to think this career was secondary to my desire for social impact. The man who offered me that job deserves someone obsessed with helicopters. My obsession is for humanity. When we were flying out teens who were already wasted drunk before noon to a community detox outfit, I knew in my soul that I would rather be the guy on the side helping get kids sober than simply deliver them to the detox facility. My gift is wringing every fibre of beauty out of life so we don't have to escape it through self-soothing ways.

I felt deep grief that this dream career was dying and that this overwhelmingly transforming adventure was not truly mine to follow. I remain endlessly grateful that the opportunity saved me $80,000 and years of commitment that I would have otherwise been blind to if not for his generous offer. However, this rule manifested in one more significant way before this journey ended.

Subtle Self-Betrayal

I was finishing my last month in Atlin before driving the thirty-seven hours to Alberta for my yearly summer volunteering for Kids Cancer Care. It felt sincere to my soul that even that epic road trip was justified for the 12 days of guiding outback life and leadership adventures for teens. I thought I was lucky to have that opportunity to give back, and I didn't flinch one bit about the distance I needed to go for it.

As I was fortunate enough to have this woman with whom I had reignited a spark before I left, things came to an abrupt halt a mere seven days before I returned home. Even though it was at a distance, there was a building tension and excitement to come back and celebrate this wild ride with somebody—the only person—I kept in touch with so deeply. That sort of intimate support sustained my spirit, and it was so helpful to have somebody who truly understood my values to navigate all this.

In the absence of that anticipation and that mental and emotional support, I defaulted to staying 'busy' to keep my mind from grieving. The best friend I had made there had just gotten his parents to fly all the way from Germany to this tiny northern village to see the new life he had grown with his partner. They invited me out to go boating and hike to the Llewellyn Glacier.

"No, no, thank you, though," I said, assuming my boss desperately needed me on this quiet day on the helipad.

If I was not working on the helicopters, I would be building the new crew cabins. My friend Alex expressed his sadness that I was 'too busy' and couldn't join what my gut knew was going to be an *incredible* day.

I caught myself saying, "No, they need me here today." As I was grieving this relationship, I assumed that I wanted to be in a narrative that I was 'needed' somehow.

Then, reflecting on the value that brought me this epic adventure, I realized I didn't even ask my boss if they 'needed' me today. I had just worked 17 days straight and was buying into my bullshit, and my soul was screaming about it.

I went to ask my boss if he was opposed to me joining Alex and his family for the adventure, and he said, "Yeah, man! It's crazy if you don't!"

Holy shit. I bought my own bullshit again.

I was so sad that I had determined my labour value as a 'safe space' to grieve and stay busy. But I was rejecting myself and what I really wanted to do. It was as if I didn't deserve to play if suddenly something fell out of order, and I was taking ownership of 'if this didn't work, neither should this other joy that I wish to feel.'

I rushed to my trailer, ripped out of my work clothes and texted them.

They hadn't left yet!

The enthusiasm in my spirit returned, and I realized I had almost let my sadness bleed over into the other joy, trying to invite itself into my life.

This day remains my favourite day of the entire northern experience.

I helped Alex, his partner, and his parents set off on their boat to the glacier. The glassy lake, the pristine wild and the incredible company... I felt like I hopped dimensions from 'woe is me' to 'look how fucking lucky I am. Look what amazing friends I've made. Look what a beautiful world we've been given.'

It was all on the other side of my self-soothing and subtle self-rejection.

At one point, the only way forward was to take off our hiking shoes and trek barefoot through a marshy creek to get into the wide-open valley. The novelty of Alex's parents trusting the ridiculousness of this wild new normalcy of life left them in awe. We shared in the laughter and audacity of it all. We guided them where to hop over creeks and built rock paths to keep their boots dry.

We propped on a perch and enjoyed lunch, taking in the magnitude of hundreds of feet of ice slowly cracking away into the lake on this summer day. We took a long way boating home and stopped to fish as much as possible, luckily snagging one small salmon on the tail end. There were at least four 'first' experiences that that friendship and that day offered me alone.

If anything, I feel that story is more significant than the grand opportunity of the piloting career. That is a once in a lifetime, whereas the sorrow of an ending relationship bleeding into the joy of other opportunities is far more common and sinister. Everyday grieving can stifle so much opportunity. But missing out on the love, friendships and potential right in front of us despite that is a failure most fowl! There can be so much goodness and people willing to shock you out of your grief if we only make ourselves receptive to it.

Every moment is pregnant with the next.

This discovery was that the injustice we do upon ourselves has momentum. Sorrow has momentum. Buying into sorrow betrays the momentum of joy in our lives. But audacity and courage have momentum, too. Courage to question our beliefs. Courage to expand our boldness. Courage to feel something new.

This book is for those who want to reclaim their boldness, for those who aren't afraid to feel and make magic of our exquisite sorrows, for those who want a story-worthy life, and for those who know that their growth is the greatest gift we can give those around us.

This is the great pursuit of owning the human experience and stacking goodness for those after us. To be pissed off with a purpose is to live with the audacity of Pronoia: What if we lived as if our bravery rewarded us with a sort of beauty and experience beyond our imagination?

We cannot know until we give it the benefit of the doubt to surprise us. We must act and let the momentum of this intricately connected world respond in unique, challenging and unforgettable ways.

Life is ready when you are.

CHAPTER 4

Imposter Syndrome

Would you be better off if you could be ignorant of your insecurities? Would you consider yourself lucky to focus on the most productive part of yourself? Even if the world could look and see what might merit insecurity, you have no obligation to agree. Is it necessary or even virtuous to understand thoughts that belittle your worth? I'd argue that it *is* valuable to be conscious of the intricacies of self-sabotage and how fear dominates our lifestyle.

I once heard that Jordan Peterson studied authoritarianism and evil for two decades. Focusing so much time and attention on such dark topics led him to admit that he 'almost didn't come back from it.' I didn't understand what that meant until I obsessively studied insecurity for a year after publishing *An Arsenal of Gratitude*.

After waging war on mediocrity and regret, I thought the next honourable fight was to wage war on insecurity. In studying gratitude, I had to research grief and all that keeps us from recognizing and maximizing the goodness in our lives. If I could be an architect of perspective, I would love to outsmart my sense of inferiority. But first, I would have to understand and validate my inferiority to know what I'm genuinely contending with, right? How could I say I won the battle if I was oblivious to the supposed 'insecurity' I was fighting?

In compiling my list of flaws, insecurities, shortcomings, misdeeds, and failures, I was actively empowering those aspects. My intent in taking an honest inventory of what I considered my own frailties was to help others feel understood and conquer inadequacy. The sinister thing about this process, though, was that *I had to buy into my own inadequacy.*

I thought I would take on the perspective of a comedian who uses his shortcomings to his advantage. If I can own my flaws and even make light of them, I have stolen anybody else's power to use my insecurities against me. It's in the attempt to hide them that the insecurity is empowered.

Back to the idea of momentum, it was profoundly empowering to dedicate my life to studying and embodying gratitude for three years. I wrote my most compelling offering on how it can become a spiritual compass for purpose and a spiritual weapon against grief. I was crafting a life-sized argument about living wholeheartedly, which manifested through my efforts. So, when I was crafting a life-sized argument for my inadequacy, it manifested through the effort. I intellectualized myself right into a depressive state. Know thy enemy, right? *Sheesh.*

I had at least three people who I trusted to understand the intimate details of my attempt to wage war on insecurity. I was pitching them my *professional* list of excuses and insecurities so I could get a rise out of them. It is my job as a writer to evoke emotion, of course. So, at that moment, I wanted to be validated for my reasons for feeling insecure. In other words, to co-sign my bullshit.

They refused.

I argued, "Then maybe you don't get it because- "

They interrupted, "No, *you* don't get it." Each of them responded in the same manner, individually, on separate occasions.

"People who love you don't see these things. And even if they do, it's surely not the focus. You are so much more than what you are trying to outrun."

The last sentence reverberated like a meteor striking a lake. Each wave ripples from my mind's core and out to my ears, repeating, *'You are so much more than the things you are trying to outrun.'*

As you can tell, I was a *ye of little faith*, as I wouldn't have to mention multiple friends if I listened right the first time. That's just good science, right? Don't base your entire belief on one instance of results. But the results were unfailingly repeatable from sources of genuine love.

Oh, look, love beats the absolute snot out of fear once again. Fear quakes in love's presence. But not loving yourself walls away other's attempts to reach you.

The buy-in of my insecurities insinuated that all those in my life have found and agreed with my worst perspective of myself. That is the subconscious effort of disarming others' love towards us before it even has a chance to reach us.

People who love you sincerely don't give a fuck about your inadequacy. They wonder why you aren't focusing on your gifts and using them to your advantage. Even if your flaws are apparent, so are the best parts of you if YOU buy into your gifts.

De Sidere

How have we come this far and not understand that our lens of the world is crafted by desire? If all of life's information is equivalent to the number of grains of sand, we only hold one handful. But we yell at each other as if we hold it all simultaneously.

When I am on a road trip, and my stomach grumbles, the next small town's spotlight is entirely on what restaurants it has. My fear is the pain of hunger. When my car makes a sketchy sound, all I can see are mechanic shops. My fear is a loss of control of my transportation. Whatever threatens me, even if self-imposed, is my focus's primary filter and desire to manage.

The essence of a *primary* desire means that others are secondary, and thirdly, after that. If we could only take a few moments and see intuitions for what they are, we would understand a substantial bit more of ourselves. If you don't know what you want, you are in one of the most interesting places a person can be: *The beginning* of everything else.

Seeds of plants and trees flip and flop across the earth until they get stuck somewhere. They then attempt to produce their full potential with whatever environment nature offers. Humanity is terrifyingly similar. Except you are the seed with legs and a free will to go and plant yourself where your full potential can manifest. Landing somewhere by accident seems rather an insult to your intelligence.

Do you think those countless seeds set loose to the earth know what they are meant to do? A fraction of those seeds even gets a chance to take root. Even fewer become something of magnitude before meeting some inconvenient or premature end. Imagine how little, yet vital information, it has to fulfill its mission. Yet, it finds a way. Another parallel is that millions of sperm all race for only the single of countless competitors to succeed. Even then, that race rarely enough even has a victor of all.

Now, here you are… against all odds, you exist. With these strange yearnings, you are fascinated and inspired by only a handful of things in an endless world of possibilities. It's not much, but it's enough to start.

The last paragraph had me curious to ask the World Wide Web, "Do sperm know where to go?"

They *friggin* do!

The unfathomably small creation, far too small for the human eye to even see, is smart enough to know where to expand its potential. Without getting too scientific, the sperm swim towards a higher concentration of molecules closer to the egg where there is more warmth. A higher concentration of molecules means *more difficult* to swim. Not open space of less resistance. The most primal of all sensations written into the *smallest* fibre of our being tells us to defy the odds and move against resistance.

So, what are we really contending with as fully grown, intelligent beings? The doubt that we are capable? Is the effort worthwhile? If you're at least as smart as a sperm, you don't know if it was worthwhile until you break through and find out, do you?

We often say dumb (inefficient) people are less hesitant in their actions. Would you rather be so intelligent as to psych yourself out of ever acting because you can see the odds are unsure? Or would you rather be more courageous because your curiosity was stronger than your caution? Neither option sounds so great, but the balance of intelligent and radical action is the sweet spot of powerful action. Sometimes, the moment needs one more than the other. But, if you are so smart, why are you so afraid?

Knowing the odds are against us but striving despite the consequences is the spirit of all evolution. It is *the* breakthrough energy that creates life itself. Why would it be any different or more complicated for this bizarre life we didn't ask for? We don't need to know how it ends; we only need to have a reason compelling enough to start the adventure. It can be as simple as realizing that doing nothing is worse than never knowing what's out there, good or bad.

Just one singular ounce of aim towards anything meaningful enough for you to *start* is all that is needed. You *are* an imposter. We all are. We are imposing ourselves into this world. We all have a right to it. The consistent course correction of gathered wisdom allows the journey to perpetuate more intelligently. We are all scared aliens trying to find a purpose and place here. If we can learn to listen to the intelligence within our own body and mind, it will nudge us all along the way.

Your hunger will tell you when to refuel, but your health will guide you in finding the *best* fuel. Your wounds will tell you when to slow down and not agitate the recovery, but your scars will remind you that you're built for the fight. Your irritations will help you navigate avoiding conflict, but your sense of justice will guide you to the conflicts worth bleeding for. Your sorrow will teach you the true value of something, but your gratitude will allow you to live out your appreciation before it's too late. Your dopamine will teach you how to play and consume the world's riches, but your serotonin will teach you how to love and share it. Your inkling of curiosity will help you follow what feels good today, while passion will help you follow the legacy you leave behind.

I began with fantasy books and would have loved to succeed in the entertainment industry. But the pain of that not taking off as well as hoped inspired the clarity that philanthropy was more in alignment with my true desires. I was more willing to continually fail in this realm of bettering myself and others. I decided the risk/reward was something I could follow for a lifetime.

So far, so good! I doubt this will ever end, as I'm annoyingly passionate about the human experience and potential, yet my story has barely begun. My desires will shift and twist until the day I die. I have nothing else going on that is more fulfilling than seeing how it all fits my personal calling and what I'm willing to risk finding out. Everything else is a bonus material to refine, nurture, and celebrate that journey along the way.

Returning to that Latin term of desire, *'De Sidere,'* to be 'from the stars,' we are figuratively and spiritually reaching for the heavenly body. If we conspire with the same strange, beautiful, harmonious wisdom of the heavenly body, then our strange and quirky ways bring the heavenly experience here, wouldn't they?

I want my life to be a living example: you can have whatever you want if you are willing to make the right and *full* sacrifices. Yet, I can only do so many things well within my finite time. With that, I assume great respect for the fact that I am not promised any definite amount of time, as my upbringing among young cancer survivors made this unmistakably evident. So, I feel called to draw as much joy and magic from the simplicity of the present moment and make what is before me as desirable as possible. It is all I ever have and perhaps ever will. I am ever so lucky if I am to stay long enough to outlive my blessings and stumble upon new ones.

There is nothing wrong with being a multi-faceted person with various joys and desires to chase. But you can only nurture so much at once. You can either have a few things of epic quality or have a bunch of half-finished projects and wonder why you lack a sense of completion. The cost of doing one thing exceptionally is the cost of all other options. I didn't make the rules; I just tried to bend them and got terrible whiplash. So, let my cautionary tale be that it is riskier never to take a real risk. You might be alive, but your soul will shrivel well before your body does.

Impose Yourself

By definition, when you enter unknown territory, you are an impostor. You are imposing yourself into something that is a foreign experience. It's called 'Day One'. Impostor syndrome as an emotion is perhaps the most accurate and obvious sensation of all. It is a direct tearing of your identity to take on a new knowing and expand yourself into a brave new adventure. Do you know who never feels impostor syndrome? People who aren't trying new things. Impostor syndrome might be the clearest sensation that you or your work is evolving.

Imposter Syndrome

Anybody who has ever started a new job is an impostor to the industry. I sure didn't want it to be obvious that it was my first day making pizza at age fourteen at Pizza Hut or deep-frying my first batch of chicken at KFC at age fifteen. But as far as the customers were concerned, I was a professional, right? As soon as we put on a uniform or claim a title, we assume authority in a certain space and feel the need to act as such.

We try to fake it until we make it. Or we could face it until we ace it. Learning by mistakes is unnecessary when we have the humility to ask those ahead of us to bestow their years on us. They might even be flattered to pay their years forward to the next in line. It validates their capabilities. Literally everybody wins when we are honest with how much help we need to start. But we *must* start.

I was an impostor as a camp counsellor, security guard, construction worker, machine operator, horseback guide, author, narrator, and so on. I had to assume capability during every first-time scenario that scared the heebie-jeebies out of me. The big difference in making new and unique steps in life is to stop consulting cowards on the topic of courage. We shouldn't validate a couch potato's opinion on backpacking abroad. When we ask people's perspectives on following in their footsteps, we should pay close attention to how much they smile while speaking on the subject. Their honesty and excitement for you are written on their face. Especially when somebody tells you how difficult something is about to be, they will assure you the worthiness of a battle worth fighting.

I sincerely hope you feel like an impostor quite often in your life. It proves you can enter foreign spaces and eventually not be a foreign object. Dancing with strangers in Mexico didn't make it obvious I was a stranger. It made it obvious that we weren't so different. Everybody you have ever loved was once a stranger. Every favourite song and meal you cook was once unknown to you. The flavours of life are far too vast for any one of us ever to taste them all ourselves.

That doesn't mean we aren't worthy. it means it is important for us to decide what flavours and experiences are worth savouring.

You haven't met all the people who will love you yet. You must say hello to strangers.

You won't find your new favourite day in the routine you've always followed. You must practice flexibility and spontaneity to welcome everything that tries to find its way into your life.

You haven't seen what you're fully capable of yet. How do I know? You're not dead yet. You are fucking *free,* and it's ridiculous if you want to convince yourself otherwise. Please, take up space. Impose yourself. Treat every person as if they know something you don't and you will listen in a way that you believe something amazing could fall out of them. To treat them with such curiosity is exactly how you inspire their sense of value to come forth.

Your conclusions about the world are an insult to everything it has yet to offer you. You must impose yourself and get lost in strange places as often as possible if you are ever to have a chance at having a valid opinion. To end this, I will offer the four rules I have written beside my bed as the first thing I see every morning so I know who I am and how to direct myself in this life.

1. Show up, work hard.
2. Help as many people as humanly possible.
3. Take every opportunity to be uncomfortable.
4. If you want it, go fucking get it.

The end.

CHAPTER 5

There Are No Dumb Questions

If it is not safe for us to scrutinize each other's ideas, we can't kill off the stupid parts of ourselves.

Monkeys prune each other to cleanliness. Trees are pruned for optimal health and potential. Snakes shed their skin and are more vulnerable in the process of being able to grow. So yes, it will be very particular, personal, probably painful and provocative to our pride to prune off our stupid parts.

If our stupid parts don't die, then we play stupid games and win stupid prizes. Your whole life can change when you ponder these foundational questions:

- What game of life am I playing? For what prize and at what cost?
- Who benefits the most from this game?
- What does it mean to be 'losing' at this game?
- Do I even like this game?
- Did I choose this game, or was it assumed by the others that I would like to partake?
- Have I considered other games life offers to expand my understanding of what is available?

There is no way I was the only kid who thought babies had to be born out of butt before I knew girls had... you know. I was just allowed to be ignorant until the education system or the world figured I could handle basic human biology. Biology is not a scary topic. Being ignorant of biology is more disturbing than anything. When we create taboos and fog around the basic things, we end up *deeply* in ignorance when we are called to love and understand imperfections, malfunctions and insecurities that bodies may produce as we grow and age.

A dumb question is an oxymoron. As I said, 'stupid' is synonymous with 'inefficient.' *Therefore*, asking a question cannot be inefficient. The sole purpose of asking questions is to be more efficient. *Not* asking questions, regardless of the simplicity or brain fart of what we would call common sense, is what is stupid. People who are too insecure to ask questions are the people who make the biggest mistakes. If we don't make a safe space to ask seemingly simple questions, we are making a breeding ground for massive problems.

The second dumbest - and possibly dangerous - person in any room is one who isn't sure how to act and won't ask. The *most* stupid - and certainly most dangerous - person in a room is somebody who doesn't know how to act, won't ask, but proceeds as if they know. Imagine any kid holding a chainsaw for the first time. All that power and no respect or concept of the harm it can cause is a disaster waiting to happen. Nobody wins by assuming. How ironic that common sense is so uncommon because the assumption is that it doesn't have to be shared or spoken about? Isn't that the definition of making something less common?

If you hear a 40-year-old say, "My parents were assholes and really didn't equip me for life." Most people wouldn't pity that person as much as if a 16-year-old said that. So where is the line? The culture hasn't defined that yet, but it may freely shame the 40-year-old anyway. If there is a gap, we can fill it. Be a gem and do it. Being a part of the shaming crowd but not part of the solution amplifies discourse and insecurity in our society.

You'd think a middle-aged person would have different problems than the damage their parents left them 20 years ago. Meanwhile, there are 16-year-olds with incredible ownership and understand their parent's pain is not theirs to bear. Then, they enter the world with a mature concept of who is responsible for their own well-being. If we don't make a safe space for those supposedly past the expiry of their grace period, then we will have a nation of old people stuck with their unsupported-child mindset. They will be prolonged children in aging bodies growing deeper and deeper resentment while being shamed for not having support or basic knowledge that may never have been offered.

If we never make a conscious offering that victimhood doesn't (and shouldn't) be a way to live, then it seems a majority will keep and sustain their powerless states. Those people just become easy prey for all those who design their companies and products around covering up but never healing insecurities.

It's like letting a small cut become an infected wound because you don't want to look at it. Not only does a small thing by nature turn far worse and more uncomfortable, but everybody has to deal with your complaining of the discomfort. If you're too insecure to receive help when it's easy, it's hard to be graceful when you're desperate for aid when it's far worse due to neglect. That teaches people how to treat you like a lost cause.

Bruising your ego is a small price in the grand scheme of alternatively festering emotional wounds over a lifetime.

On a lighter note, I'm all for horseplay and making light of people's ignorance when it's for wholesome fun. For example, when I started on the pipeline in northern Alberta, we watched the welders tell their new helper to do a 'spark test.'

The welder made his helper catch the welding sparks in a Styrofoam cup and sprint to the foreman for inspection. They had to make sure the 'lead was healthy.' These new guys rush through the snow in -30°C with spark burns, hoping to gain approval. But they are just hauling ass through the snow with an empty cup.

The guy wants to earn respect and trusts that his mentors have his best interest at heart. But if his blind faith suggests no reason for threat, he has no reason to assume he is being made fun of. He might properly assume there is no wasted effort when everybody is freezing in the hellish Canadian winters. Sometimes you must be the butt of a laugh to keep morale alive. Humour is also a sign and practice of comfort among people. There is warmth in that, too.

We are valuable to one another because of the intricate gaps of wisdom and knowledge we may offer each other. We have dramatic varieties of perspective, intelligence, humour, and ingenuity to share. The fact that we don't have everything in common is where the value lies. There are entire worlds of experience hiding behind every person if we have only enough curiosity.

Learned Helplessness

People can look around and see that others are not stressed while doing things we consider stressful. That visual communication of seeing how easily people accomplish tasks helps us judge who to listen to and take advice from. Whether in relationships, professions, self-care, cooking, or anything else. On the other hand, if we see somebody visually unwell and growing irritated, we see if we can lend a hand.

Somewhere along the line, we started shaming people for not knowing better. This diminishes people's aspirations to even try, resulting in 'learned helplessness.' Not only are they disheartened, but they may cognitively reject information because the topic or task reminds them of a time when they felt so pathetic. If you are not a safe space for people to ask any question of any difficulty whatsoever, then you are prolonging the stupidity and ignorance of the world.

An example might be never being taught how to change a flat tire. But if you called for help from a parent or friend and they called you an idiot for not figuring out how to help yourself, a cascade of resentment might unfold. Not only do you feel *more* alone and helpless, but you may have a growing fear and hate towards any vehicular mechanic knowledge because of those foundational experiences. You may be able to save money by learning, but the continued unwillingness to revisit that may cost you extra in future mechanic bills.

We have a clear opportunity to minimize suffering more often than we realize. People who are belittled for taking longer than 'normal' or having any difficulty learning are then taught not to present themselves in situations where they might feel timid. This is a fast way to teach people to have small, fearful, and secluded lives.

Could you imagine if we could normalize the virtue of curiosity on a societal scale? It would be admirable to ask questions and express wonderment about everything. Oh, right, we were all like that as kids until it was stifled from us. It is our *nature* to be curious and explore, yet we have been made to feel we are burdening people in pursuit of our own exploration. Telling kids to shut up and stop being so curious is how we raise insecure adults with no sense of exploration, creativity or enthusiasm for the unknown.

Meanwhile, mankind's progress has been in the hands of the relentlessly curious and creative. Take that into consideration. Nobody who truly cares about you is going to co-sign your ignorance. Only those who have something to benefit from you staying small will advocate for your limited perspective and sense of agency over your own life.

The Intelligence All Around Us

Isn't it a little ironic if we call something common, and it becomes a thing of division? Our differences are exactly what we bring to the table to offer each other. That intelligence to be able to sit among people of different backgrounds, races, values, and goals does not have to create a threat. Those differences are the exact gift that may be what sparks evolution for one another. But it can never be accomplished by belittling their current state.

It is the patient compassion that allows people to own their experience that allows them to spread their wings. Perhaps I don't have a personal relationship enough with birds to be entirely sure about this, but my educated guess is that they do not swoop up beside each other and talk shit if a bird is falling behind. No, they fly in a v-formation because it is cooperative and maximizes communal efficiency.

Cooperation does not suggest that there is never a conflict of interest. It creates a space to negotiate so that conflict is unnecessary. There is a world of difference in conflict when you decide it is you and others united against a problem rather than the 'problem' manifesting in the other person. Even if the other person *is* the problem, you can preface that you are already a team, but the individual facet of the issue is something to conquer together and celebrate.

All conflicts in life can transform if you adopt that one perspective shift. It is not immediately easy, but it will dramatically alter the outcomes and ability to win alongside the supposed 'opposition'.

People's commitment to choose the most aggressive course of action is no longer essential in this age. Choosing violence and domination may create a solution temporarily, but it makes for generations of conflict as a long-term result. Some of us are stuck in conflicts that our granddaddies can no longer justify. We call in tradition and stop asking questions, don't we?

We subconsciously perpetuate what we don't dissect and consciously choose. So, if we don't ask why the fuck we are still fighting and if it's a reasonable thing to do, then we keep it.

We are the current definition of tomorrow's future. We can redefine traditions wherever we like and be something brand new. Our successors are just as capable and free to discard what we set in motion and make it brand new to their own. There is no shame in redefining our customs over and over until it is something we can proudly replicate.

I could never forget when my friend joked, "Traditions are just peer pressure from dead people."

We are now experiencing what all previous generations may have only dreamed of: having worldwide connection and influence in the palm of our hand. It's safe to say that few of us know how to manage that kind of power. It has swallowed many in mere hope of gaining attention, yet they've submitted to being digital slaves to other's expectations of them.

We crumble under the pressure to 'get it right.' As if there is any 'right' way about life and legacy beyond a valiant effort and desire to help the next generation do it all better. Ideally, we also experience as much joy for ourselves along the way. We can't expect anybody to want to learn or gain from us if we are resentful of our own experience. Our suffering is only in vain if we don't share and make our failures valuable information for others to avoid.

Somebody somewhere had to smoke everything, eat everything, touch everything and pay the price of curiosity. Our cautionary tales are just as valuable, if not *more* valuable, than positive choices. The wisdom of what *not* to do is a war cry of well-being that we need more now than ever to avoid perpetuated stupidity. It's only our embarrassment, ego and self-inflation to think we are beyond mistakes to not turn our blooper reel into a laugh and wisdom paid forward to limit the suffering of others. Otherwise, people we love may stumble into familiar hells from which we could have saved them if we just had a little humility.

Building Your Own Game

Other success brought us here after hundreds of generations of daily life done the best they know how. Best is always made better when we are in constant curiosity of the new and improved ways to walk about this life. The fastest way to do that is to create a space where you can be of service with your wisdom and allow others to reciprocate the gesture. Do this as often as friendships, love, and life offer.

The following chapters will shed light on how you might be playing this game and that there may be other ways to play the game of life. You can't teach others to play with you if you don't know your rules. If you can't ask others how they want to play and win, you can't expect to accidentally win a game you don't know you're even playing. Here are the questions from this chapter again to ponder:

- What game of life am I playing? For what prize and at what cost?
- Who benefits the most from this game?
- What does it mean to be 'losing' at this game?
- Do I even like this game?
- Did I choose this game, or was it assumed by the others that I would like to partake?
- Have I considered other games life offers to expand my understanding of what is available?

How do we redefine every fragment of who we are to a newer and growing definition of well-being?

A ridiculous amount of curiosity. A curiosity as large as life. Trial-and-error in the spirit of minimizing suffering and harmonizing humanity.

With a billion ways to be blind and afraid in a visionary world, the pursuit of understanding ourselves and the unlimited future must be treated like a playground. There are no dumb questions. The next time you feel nervous to ask a question, that is a first step to your expansion.

You owe it to yourself and to the benefit of all others to reignite your curiosity and playfulness in exploring this life.

Bonus Challenge

Here's a practice everybody can adopt that will stimulate curiosity and play in everyday experiences. Add this rule to your life: Every time you go to the grocery store, you must try a new product. This will shift a boring routine into the excitement of knowing that when you seek something new, it is *always* hiding in plain sight. Even greater fun is in picking a stranger to choose something for you.

You might be forced to learn to cook new food. The more you explore, the more you have to share. Weird food is one of the most undervalued experiences to share with friends and loved ones. It's emotional, flavorful and playful to share. Once you do that with food, you realize you can do it with all of life. One habit like that overflows into all other aspects, and soon, you'll grow a lens for a new flavour of life in everything.

PS: You sometimes may spend money on raunchy food and flavours. Welcome to fucking around and finding out. It's half the beauty of the unknown. But the achievement and satisfaction of expanding a skillset and way of life will justify the hilarious adventure of new flavours. It has been one of the most enjoyable ways to keep daily life fresh and exciting for myself and those I share it with.

Happy hunting!

Chapter 6

Anthem of a Life

Our personal narrative of the world is broken down into the dance of three perspectives. Sadly, perspectives are simply unique distortions of our experience. To have three of them all dancing at the same time makes for a laughable situation. That situation is lived out as our life story.

The three foundational perspectives are:

1. What is. (The Past)
2. What it ought to be. (The Present)
3. How we can make it so. (The Future)

The universal plot is 'Things are not as they seem.' This is because there are only two possibilities for the possibility of *everything*. Either everything is on purpose or nothing at all. With no way to know, we are already at odds on the heart of existence. Let's play out each mentality as if we knew it was the absolute truth.

The Universe Has Made No Mistake
Consider that every event to ever happen is faultless simply because it happened. If it would be any other way, for better or worse, that would be the purest evolution. Thousands of generations of people at their finest had brought us to this exact moment and it's perfectly fine that it took this long. The state of everything is the cause and effect of a perfectly imperfect humanity playing out its potential with

its wickedness, kindness, miracles and tragedies alike. The record of us as people at our finest and at our worst allows us to guide our future to the most ideal place. What we consider mistakes along the way are perfectly designed for exactly how long it is meant to take whether we persist or give up on our ambitions.

So why ponder what could have been when divine motion brought only what currently is? Everything will always revert to the three steps of our perception that make our unique mark in this life matter: what is, what it ought to be, and how we can make it so.

Our free will would be the only source of changing the story of history. But if our will is no mistake, then our whim and instinct are not worth arguing about either. You are just a passenger in a body with its fears and hopes. Our belief or wonder if we are free is the only variable in an otherwise perfectly unfolding reality.

If you hate the thought that you may not be free, then this book is absolutely for you.

This wonderful suggestion is that when the designer of the universe made you and your gifts, the designer factored in your stupidity. Meaning that despite your sense of inadequacy, you are perfectly designed to overcome the unique challenges that come with your life. Missteps, fumbles, and all else, the only difference is whether you nurture your chosen potential and play the finest game you can. Choosing not to play is how you would simulate being dead before you actually die. Alternatively…

The Universe is a Mistake

If this was the case, everything is basically a chemical explosion of cause and effect. Everything you do is equally likely a mistake. To live this out, you have no obligation to anything, and your freedom is paramount. Your freedom is the only experience. Everything else becomes an obstacle or the weapon of choice to satisfy your desire.

Everything will revert to the three steps of our perception that make our unique mark matter in this grand mistake. What is it, what it ought to be, and how can we make it so. You would be the universal exception and become the story of how powerful somebody of intention can be in a world of mistakes.

Either Way

See the similarity between either possibility? Both conclusions on the origin of everything still narrow down to what you will do with your time here. Cats will continue to poop outside of their litter box. People convinced of finding their soulmate will still find themselves heartbroken. People will stumble upon hobbies that turn them into rockstars, influencers, and cautionary tales.

Some people will never be convinced they are happy until a million others justify their lifestyle, while another knows its worth by how their dog looks at them. People will crawl their way out of tragic childhoods to be monks, warriors, tyrants, healers, pacifists, activists, drug dealers, philosophers, and all the other sorts of 'probably the best for me.'

The stories of everybody else are the atmosphere behind your own journey. Eight billion other people who found themselves in the same era did their own mental math of what is, what ought to be, and how they can make it so. They are all valid to their own understanding. But understanding can fundamentally change. We harmonize through values and nurture one another through shared ambitions.

You are not responsible for anybody else's decisions because the world will determine their fate. As it always has. Sometimes, it reroutes us through failure. Sometimes, it reroutes us through military force or natural disasters. Through the desires of a loved one, the avoidance of pain, the pursuit of pleasure, or a compelling stranger who told a story that changes our path. All we can do is harmonize our own ultimate orchestra of community, values and potential.

Our one and only dance is not knowing what's next and how to make it what we desire. We are fate-weavers. How we narrate our reaction and attitude to our life story is the music that emits through our soul to every other person we cross. The song that rings out from our core is what becomes the universal law of attraction. Musicians narrate and craft sound to manipulate emotion and decorate time. People overlap values and talents to manipulate their experience and decorate life's potential.

How a Song Evolves

What does it mean to hold composure? It means that despite the influences around you, that you are composing something of your own will against all odds. If a composition is a literary, artistic, or musical product, so is your life.

If a prayer is the act of celebrating, striving, or requesting a hope or wish for the future, music and prayer are virtually the same. Many religious and spiritual people say, 'The potency of prayer grows when two or more are gathered in unity.' Is music not the same? Do we not get chills down our spine to witness a thousand people who've never met unify over a chorus? Do we not feel more at home when we enter a building full of people humbled in their humanness and celebrating second chances? This is all 'What is' and 'What it ought to be' searching for connectedness in 'How we can make it so.'

Sometimes, a song eerily echoes our own experience. Both prayer and music can teach us that it's ok to celebrate being stuck between 'What is' and 'What ought to be' before we know 'How we can make it so.' This *whole* journey, even amidst the hardest times, is a worldwide dare to learn how to dance in the rain of difficulties. How can we bring humour into times that seem devoid of joy? How can we look at an emotional pain in a way that allows us to take it from the inside, put it out into the world, and call it the art of the human story?

Though, not all stories are the same. They don't have to and aren't meant to be. But when we find the art that reflects our own story, we feel less alone and get a glimpse of proof that this sorrow is not the end. It is merely a moment before the magic between 'What life ought to be' and 'How we can make it so' unfolds slightly further.

We are so captivated when it feels as if the song finds us rather than us searching for it. A prayer or song can equally break us down when we feel something smashes through our composure and makes us feel seen and understood. That is why people who can communicate well and empathize can also tear down our masks and glimpse at our core being whether we see it or not. Whether we are hiding or embracing our true state of being, the real, raw version of our souls is what is singing out into the abyss to find one another.

The mask we put on to fool others (and ourselves) into being what we are not authentically can only play so long before our lack of harmony dis-regulates our very being. Disease is literally the disorder of structure. Disorder in a way that brings malfunction to a form of life. So, lying and trying to be anything other than authentic will be how we narrate and create malfunction of our well-being. But it may only begin to form as a malfunction and lack of harmony from the external world, making us blame the world instead of ourselves.

If where we are seems fundamentally inharmonious, we must navigate chaos to find where our soul finds ease. That's where new songs with new sounds, new playstyles, and new parts of humanity emerge.

That's an adventure, baby! That's the story of evolution itself!

Co-Creation

Existence is a grand song in which we have all taken our own tunings. We find one another and clash our energy to see what parts of us can be harmonious and perhaps write a story that the world has never seen yet. Even if it is a story that has been sung for generations, some songs are meant to endure all of time. This fibre of who we are ripples forth where humanity is getting life right.

There will certainly be pressure to continue singing our parents, community, and ancestors' songs. It is not wrong or immoral to divert if it does not harm the whole. Once upon a time, we were tribes; now, we are globally connected. We can witness and expose ourselves to foreign ideas and ideals. We can mix and master the human experience on a vastness that has never been possible until now. But as potential increases, the possibility that disharmony and disease can be instilled also increases. Hopelessness that we even matter in the vastness of potential is one of those diseases.

Place yourself in atmospheres that teach new kinds of music and expose yourself to what brings forth your enthusiasm. Again, enthusiasm itself is the definition of embodying the spirit of God. Pure, authentic transmutation of honest and joyful experience. People don't need to understand exactly what they see; they need to know they are allowed to be enthusiastic and accepting of their unique expression to add to humanity's symphony. Connection and enthusiasm are an antidote to hopelessness.

The world has more songs than we can ever learn. This means some songs have not yet been sung, and stories have not yet found each other. When we clash with others in ways that amplify our best, we expose the possibility of bringing the world something it has never seen before. This can be an actual song or any way people lose themselves in the moment and harmonize with their experience. Whether it be adrenaline, creativity, humour, playing with fear, or simply playing. Meaningful connection at its core.

The difference now is that everybody can observe, but very few are involved. It's the ability to look at the whole world's menu and read the explanations but never taste the food. People think they've lived, but all they've done is eat the words on the paper and try to convince others that they've tasted life. You can't eat the whole menu like you can't experience the whole world. It takes an investment. You won't have room for all the other experiences and flavours. But at least you will have *lived*.

Just like enjoying a meal, it is richer in good company. Our company amplifies or diminishes all of life's flavours. Nobody can sustain perfect and timeless harmony. Dinner may be perfectly good, yet if a couple fights and stomps off from the meal, we say 'dinner is ruined.' The food may still be perfectly healthy. It has nothing to do with the food. It is the experience itself that is muddied by disharmony. But we blame all the other factors and forget that harmony was what the experience was built upon.

Out of Tune

The opposite tragic reality unfolds for those who were embittered to the point of losing their sense of celebration and song in life. I believe nobody intentionally goes out of their way to destroy the magic in the world. But the bitterness of others may block the possibility of a song worth singing and living out. Those people are just as hungry for connection and harmony as anybody else, but all they can hear is the negativity that is numbing the joy. These people emit tunes that are so grungy and foul that it makes living feel difficult. It is not their fault. It is just that it is all that they may have ever known or heard. Meanwhile, the tunes of love and bliss they hear in the distance and wish to learn seem out of reach.

The disheartening part is that some people are so consumed by their sorrowful and resentful songs that their zest for life nearly diminishes entirely. Let's be abundantly clear that some perfectly fine and wealthy people are just bitter. Whereas there are children who have been raised in endless dysfunction and people who have lived through true hell and haven't lost hope in goodness.

Those with a lost connection to goodness metaphorically turn off their radio signal. This means neither good nor bad can enter. Yet, they are so consumed by negativity that it becomes their only operative sensation. Every continued experience of agony amplifies their belief in a wicked and broken world—not for lack of effort but of repetitive proof (thus far) that their hope was misplaced and mishandled time and time again.

Even if a good thing is presented and offered, their receptivity has turned off. This is what brings up one of my favourite quotes:

'Those who were seen dancing in the rain were considered insane by those who could not hear the music.' - Friedrich Nietzsche

Our stories and songs never stop singing whether we like it or not. Our vibration is begging to be heard, connected and evolved. Much like the roots of a tree slowly but surely break through concrete and overwhelm everything around it by the pure nature of its expansion. We are very much the same. It is our story of 'What is,' 'What ought to be,' and 'How we make it so.' Those who've turned off their reception and closed themselves to life's offerings are the equivalent of a plant cutting off its own branches every time it threatens to bloom.

Everybody's fight for a story worth telling is equally right to survive and grow as it harmonizes potential with others worldwide. The saddest song to hear is a life's light stomped out on its own accord well before it gave the world the opportunity to change its story.

There are new songs to sing. There are new instruments to play. New games to play. New tools to forge a life like no other.

There are new people to meet whose harmony can and has endured hell.

If you're going to receive what this book has to offer properly, I need you to turn your receptivity on that goodness is alive and fucking well. And it's trying to find you. It's trying to see what you're made of. It wants to see your story out to the bitter end. It wants you to hear the reverberating heartbeat of people who don't quit because the going got tough.

The music will always be playing in the hearts of those who refuse to surrender to sorrow and grief. In fact, it is in the presence of sorrow and grief that the music is truly *felt*. It is how we act like a living prayer and bargain with the future against all odds. We are fucking magnificent. And you are welcome to come dance in the rain with us who refuse to play small and live silently. Bring all your flaws, your fuck ups, your insecurities and your grievances.

Love fears no fractured past. Grace does not flinch at your fumbles and your failings. Forgiveness stares you in the eyes, waiting for you to get out of your own way. Courage is built into our beating hearts, wondering when you'll join the anthem of a life worth living.

The world has no intention to make you less afraid. I swear to God, if you dare to move despite every reason you think you must cower, the world will rejoice in being reminded…

There is *bravery* in this world.

Chapter 7

Echoes of Cain

Why would we perpetuate a struggle if we can win the game forever by annihilating the enemy? But then, what game is there left to play if you have nobody to play with? And why serve a God if you can kill him and become your own instead?

My first lesson in revenge was the biblical story of Cain and Abel. This murder was not rooted in justice but in jealousy and insecurity.

Shortly put, the first two biblical children of humanity, born from Adam and Eve, were asked to give a sacrifice by fire unto God. Abel offered up his firstborn lamb, which was a great deal in comparison to Cain's offering of fruit. The bonfire- apparently the embodied spirit of God here - accepted the lamb with great fervour and blazed heavily. Afterwards, the fire seemed to smoulder and dwindle in response to Cain's offering, communicating that Abel's offering was superior.

Cain had consulted with God and received the message that his sacrifice was not as worthy. If Cain was to be the less favoured under the eyes of his creator, he did not respond by upping his offering but by slaying his brother.

In this instance, have you ever felt rejected and that there was not enough love to go around? Then you have felt what Cain felt. Have you ever felt like your contribution is under-appreciated? Then you have felt what Cain felt. Have you ever felt that your effort was fruitless? Then you have felt what Cain felt.

Abel did exactly what was asked - perhaps not knowing it was to be a competition - and was slain by his own brother for doing the right thing. How often are we belittled or looked down upon for being happy or enthusiastic about our own lives? A sinister and sad part of us would find pleasure in seeing another's prosperity stomped out. Only in pure hopelessness would we seek to feel less alone by tarnishing other's joy.

We all have a little bit of the spirit of Cain. We all experience sorrow so profound in the injustice we experience and witness through life. Rage is perhaps the easiest thing to feel in this world where the first children of Earth couldn't believe their God had enough favour to go around. That was when there were less than ten people in the entire world. Now, 7.8 billion people roam this broken paradise looking for love and acceptance.

How do I *know* that we are looking for love and acceptance? Because the opposite of love is *fear*. Love didn't guide Cain's reaction. The fear and assumption that there was not *enough* love prompted his violent reaction. That fear and anguish of rejection is so soulfully painful that it led a man so astray as to kill his brother.

Cain was given an ample warning that 'sin crouched at his door.' Cain did not consult his creator but was warned nonetheless and followed the sinister calling of his hardened heart.

The story finalizes as Cain and his children are marked with a curse and cast out by God. This curse declared that anybody who took revenge on Cain would suffer sevenfold. This might suggest that vengeance is simply a multiplier of suffering. It is the epitome of playing a stupid game to win a stupid prize.

Cain's innocence is arguable as no human had yet ever died. He had no idea how much pain he could inflict. Therefore, in the limited details, the lesson drawn might be that malicious, selfish intent can bring out the pain and suffering unfathomable until it is acted out. Therefore, instead of inflicting further pain, a threat of greater atrocity had to be enough to stop rage in its wake. In fact, God twisted fear itself to a higher ideal. When proper retribution does not seem in sight, limiting stupidity will have to do.

For those of us like Abel who are simply doing what we believe to be proper and harmonious, we must also grow bold enough to fend off those with hardened hearts. We must grow meaner than evil.

Why Values Matter

The effects of both love and fear ripple out with power beyond our measuring. We can only choose which to respond with and build our lives on. Love, paired with the appropriate fear of our capacity for selfishness and cruelty, is how we can stay balanced.

War is man's failure as an intelligent creature. No matter what heritage you believe runs through your veins, we have a history of mankind desperately seeking their Creator's favour. You and I have both - willingly or unwillingly – sought a higher power's favour. Whether that was our blood-creators (Parents), a divine creator, or whatever ideal inspired us. Our common thread is that violence arises wherever harmony fails to be negotiated. It's a wicked attempt to create harmony by eliminating the adversary.

When we are incapable of self-regulation as children, we have temper tantrums and get destructive when we don't have our way. But when we are grown and capable of regulating ourselves, we must have values and ideals that overpower our destructive and selfish side. Sometimes, the reality is that we don't get our way for years on end, and hopelessness seeps into our spirit. The resentful spirit of Cain can bloom in a world blanketed in injustice.

When it feels like God or goodness itself has abandoned us, fear and wrath never save the day. Love, grace, and servitude in raising one another up can end that suffering. However, God gave his angels weapons because not all wars are won with patience and understanding. So, we must create ourselves as people who operate out of love yet are meaner than evil.

When Love is Misplaced

It was built in our nature to obsess over our fear and rejection. When denied and cast away, we tap into a side of us that is hellbent on ending that pain. The sensation of inadequacy can bring out terrible sides of us that are the equivalent of a faulty creation. Like an impurity, we want to annihilate it to consider ourselves in the closest likeness to a perfect creator. This comes with an obsession with compensating for our insecurities. Little do we realize this only accentuates our insecurity's effect on us.

In the obsessive pursuit of masking our pain, we lose the humility that allows us to truly be understood and connect back to love. When we predetermine a part of ourselves as unlovable or unworthy, it's like burying a landmine in a garden you build with your loved ones. One wrong step, miscommunication or joke and it feels like irreparable damage has been done. But rarely do we own that we are the ones who have agreed to our own sense of inadequacy and the destructiveness of those feelings if provoked.

Some of the self-defeating ways we have responded to broken spiritual, parental or intimate relationships have manifested in a likeness to murder. Not physical murder, but in our hearts and minds. If harmony with others seems hopeless, that desire for servitude to a higher power can grow spiteful and become self-serving as a last resort.

If we are not actively participating in the wholeness of ourselves and others, then our passivity and resentment play into the discourse of it all. There is no middle passive ground. We are either for love and amplify it in ourselves and others, or we participate in its apathy.

If we replace a harmonious ideal with the value of selfish pleasures, we can convince ourselves that we are our own god. Whatever you serve is your god. So, if you feel so wronged by the world that you think love is corrupt and just a means to capitalize on you, you participate in that same act.

To be your own god, you must be mighty enough to try and make others feel lesser than you while being resentful enough to convince yourself that it is a righteous way of being. Some are rejected so deeply that they must create a world where they are their own highest power. This is not as rare as you think. It's basically the essence of any narcissist, abuser, manipulator or tyrant.

Every false god (or narcissist) needs somebody to worship them, or their power is moot. But adoration inspired by fear or manipulation is no adoration at all. What 'god' would they be if nobody was coming to validate them? One who has proven themselves not worth worshiping. But love and worship are two different things. I may be forced to worship somebody who holds my only means of survival, but begging for my well-being is not love. Love is of pleasant selflessness.

One of the scariest things is how the word 'love' can be weaponized against us. 'Love' can masquerade as people acting selfless and offering favours, only to use that as leverage to demand your time or favours in return. That is mere manipulation.

People who make themselves false gods stop seeing others as equal. If they intend to be the highest power in their world, you cannot hope for them to empower you. These people maintain their importance by keeping you reliant and feeling incapable without them. They are like a boss at work who loves your labour yet takes the credit for your job. They also intentionally keep you ignorant enough never to be able to replace them.

Be wary of people who act as if they have exclusive access to higher wisdom and speak on its behalf. People can give themselves moral immunity by suggesting their stance is that of a higher power, and all others are inferior and 'lost' for arguing with them. It's one thing to stand firm in a belief, but another to believe that all others are 'lost' or 'astray' for not having the same belief or complex as them.

People like this love to give answers about what is good for you without ever asking what *you* desire. Those who want you to have ultimate ownership and empowerment of your life will guide you through *your* intuition. They will not point at a path and demand you walk it.

Love Never Hurt You

Let's get real; love isn't what messed you up. Love did not manipulate you. Love didn't make you feel unappreciated. Love didn't traumatize you. Love didn't feed your anxiety. Love didn't make you feel inadequate. Those who operate by their *fear* did that to you. Despite all of that, love will mend these wounds.

I am just one man. I cannot play every role I know is needed in the world. But if my own spirit can be redeemed through the love and grace of others when I believe I deserved it the least, what an absolute privilege to pay such a priceless gift forward. Like an abused puppy, we may snap and be wary of a genuine loving hand. It requires patience and grace to earn the trust of the wounded. Yet, like that wounded puppy, we yearn to lean into being cared for and reciprocate that love.

The God that I serve *is* love. Serving 'love' in this world is my attempt to empower others to be maximally courageous, intelligent, healthy and authentic. I think justice in this world is playing and competing with others at their maximum potential. Like watching world sports, we want the best and most capable people to team up and challenge each other. It demands incredible diligence and effort, but it's thrilling to witness.

I want the same for all of you. But not just in one facet. I want to see your entire existence maximized. I want you to be so convinced and clear of your value that your own self-love inspires your full actualization, no matter the weird and wonderful ways that will manifest and challenge you.

To do that, you will inevitably be forced to harmonize with others. *Because* you alone can only go so far. With harmonized ambitions alongside others, you will not merely leap forward but soar.

All the while, the resentful spirit of Cain will remain in others. They will try to grab at your heels and prevent you from flying because their own emotional wings have been clipped. I am not deluded that purely malicious and selfish people prowl around every corner. Serving love demands that I also learn how to defend it.

Forgiveness alone does not balance a world where some believe vengeance is justice. Forgiveness merely interrupts the momentum of maliciousness yet still leaves victims. We also need altruism to be the opposite of vengeance.

If vengeance is the momentum of maliciousness, then altruism must be the momentum of love. We must soften ourselves into love yet strengthen our body and spirit to fend off those with hardened hearts. Like wounded puppies, those with the spirit of Cain may be so fearful and resentful that they never soften for the loving hand that reaches for them. Those puppies grow into feral dogs that prey on those with poor boundaries. We will have no choice but to be bigger and meaner than them on behalf of love.

My Obsession

Why am I obsessed with gratitude, emotional intelligence, and paying love forward? The 2019 stats of North America suggest that *both* suicides and overdoses *individually* overtook car crashes in fatalities.[i] We are killing ourselves faster than everything other than old age and 'preventable' causes. The worst part? That is the statistics in 2019, the year before COVID-19, where suicides multiplied *fivefold*.

The world's malice is so evidently rampant that *hopelessness* is a leading cause of death in what we claim is the most abundant era in history. How have we become materialistically rich yet communally and intimately starved?

Many who are not compelled to engage in outward violence will turn it inward. Some people believe their suffering and sorrows are justified by their imperfections and mistakes. The redeeming qualities of unconditional love are how we may serve one another to shatter those self-destructive beliefs. I will share how I, myself, am living proof in the next chapter.

We are deeply designed for this crazy journey. We are nothing but hope and bravery paved through generation over generation. We now live in an age where sorrow, loneliness and lack of purpose are our greatest threats. Your love and enthusiasm for life is a war cry that is desperately needed more than ever.

Gratitude for what we have makes optimism sustainable.

Humility levels the playing field. We are all connected and interdependent on this strange and beautiful journey.

Love allows us to be fragile and afraid and still fucking powerful. Our vulnerability and fear are what make it interesting.

Our enthusiasm and creativity are how we let the overflow of our expression sow itself into the world. We are all written into eternity.

Bravery allows us to contend with creation and terror itself. It allows our suffering to be justified and be endured to meaningful matters. Tragedies and misfortunes are made more bearable in the camaraderie of others. In practicing a unified purpose with our friends and loved ones today, tomorrow's children will witness hope in motion.

As we master our experience, we can offer more to each other and those after us. We transform our woes into wisdom and sorrows into survival guides. We bring momentum to humanity. As we grow stronger and meaner than evil, we create a home safe enough that our universal story moves forward and our anthem of bravery echoes through time.

The rest of this book will cover ways our fear and insecurity have been misshapen and weaponized against us. I will cover ways our life force and natural magnificence are being harvested without us realizing it. I will shed light on subtle ways we undermine ourselves and how we can regain the momentum of courage. I will shatter societal stigmas and prove that we are anti-fragile. Our magnificence can grow with each tribulation.

We are taking our power and our future back.

Chapter 8

I Could Be a Cowboy... Or Batman!

One of the longest-shared family memories is one between my middle brother, Lorne, and me. In the early 2000s, when we were too young to be bugged by the internet, our shenanigans had simple inspirations. What we thought was possible was as vivid as the last movie we watched. If we saw a hero, we wanted to be like that.

Having grown up in a rural area with horses, my brother knew deepest in his core that he would be a cowboy. That came true for all of us, but that manifested in funny ways as six- and eight-year-old kids. See, having found my joy in video games after living in the hospital for a month during cancer treatments, I was captivated by different inspirations. I liked my knights and dragons. He liked his cowboys, horses, and wild ingenuity to make the most of what little a cowboy might have.

On any casual day, I would be playing a game or walking out of the basement room as Lorne had been waiting all along with a lasso ready to try to rope me. Often, he would end up giving me terrible rope burns around my neck or ankles. One of these times in particular, he had got the ropes around my ankles and started dragging me across the floor despite my cries of pain.

Needless to say, I told Mom.

Shortly after, Lorne watched his first Batman movie. He was captivated by how a man could hang upside down and swoop in to save the day. Lorne had wrapped his lasso around the ceiling railings in our basement, climbed the couch, tied the opposite end to his ankles and took a great leap. That sucks for him because he was great at tying knots.

He found himself dangling upside down by the ankles, not strong enough to reach up and save himself. I was in the near room playing on the computer when I heard his cries for help. I came out to see how he got himself stuck and was very pleased, considering my fresh rope burns. I laughed and left without going for help.

An hour or two later, our father had come downstairs to find his son hanging upside down from the roof. If I remember, I think he got mad at me for not helping him, but I told him he deserved it for roping me. The whole circumstance was so absurd that he couldn't help but laugh. Especially when Lorne had to explain he watched Batman once and was sure he could do the same. Talk about the power of influence!

No Price Goes Unpaid

Two decades later, Lorne remains a cowboy down to the core and has a family that joyfully follows the same footsteps. He might still try to be Batman occasionally, but he doesn't tell anybody about it. Between what seems like his childhood and his rightful place on this earth (for now, anyway), plenty of filler moments were just as significant. Most of us go through a common thread of experiences that are vaguely common to the core but hide all the profound details that lead to our future choices.

We start life with blurry outlines of ideals and heroes. Barbie dolls for girls and toy soldiers for boys. But nobody is portraying to kids that real-life Barbies can end up with body dysmorphia and real-life soldiers can end up with PTSD. Nobody wants to ruin playtime for kids by explaining that. And I'm *certainly* not advocating for that.

but we begin aspiring towards ideals and heroism without understanding the full scope of the cost and consequences.

I think all of us talk about caricatures of careers but rarely, if ever, paint fully detailed pictures of what it is like to live out that pursuit. Some people want to be paramedics to help the sick and injured. A noble aspiration, right? But the gruesome scenes and emotionally traumatic crossfire of grieving loved ones are not on the marketing billboard for aspiring paramedics, is it?

We have a low-resolution understanding of people's jobs and lifestyles. We typically have the dumbed-down and romanticized versions in our head. So, we do not know how to communally tend to those who are following paths and are shaken to their core and fundamentally changed by their pursuit of an honourable career.

Case in point: My father as a Royal Canadian Mounted Police Officer.

Most young boys have a God complex attached to their father, considering they are as much their creator as whatever actual 'creator' we end up believing in. We are convinced our parents are infallible, intentional and calculated in every move. The boldness and the brokenness create our concept of human goodness and personal potential. We had a father who had honourable recognitions for literally running into burning buildings and saving people. That is cookie-cutter heroism at its finest. He danced with devastation and is the reason others are better off because of it.

"We want to be a cop like you, Dad!" We said.

"No, you don't." He declared. "Maybe a firefighter, a teacher... a *cowboy*." No surprise, guess who taught us how to be cowboys?

"Why can't we be like you?" We asked.

I'm pretty sure he always managed to sidestep well enough not to admit daily events that eventually lead to PTSD. It wasn't to be rude but to protect us from how hard it is to be a hero and come home as if nothing terrible happened. He did a damn good job of that and is still one of the toughest humans I've ever met after a lifelong dedication to his heroism. Shadowing our creator the best we could, we sons all adopted a common characteristic of not knowing how to welcome our loved ones into what's twisting us inside.

Yeah, we're convinced it's the courageous, manly thing to do.

Bear the greatest weight you can and bear it well. We're convinced nobody can see what's weighing on us. However, it ripples through our relationships as a crossfire of things we are too afraid to face. Ironic, isn't it?

Who's out there teaching the heroes that it's ok to be hurt? Who's out there mending the minds of heroes who were consumed by the hell they fended off for us? Or merely the hell this life has put us all through? Sorrow, grief, and trauma do not discriminate. Some kinds of grief are so deeply woven into us that we sow it into our identity in every way we can without revealing the tragedy itself. There are younger versions of us frozen in time, stalled out in the dire moments. Memory has a death grip on our nervous system to ensure we see the signs of such a foul sensation ever coming near again.

We can follow every reasonable step along a worthwhile path and be completely transformed in ways that go against our will and best efforts. We cannot undo what has been experienced; we can only live forward to the best of our ability. It is the supposed unspeakable things that hold the most power over us. Those things put us at a stalemate of growth. A story cannot continue to unfold and find a new ending if we are afraid to face the true details of our story so far.

Our Half-Written Story

Once upon a time, my brother did not know who Batman was. The next day, he *was* Batman. Not necessarily a *good* batman, but a boy who did Batman stuff. Why do we find ourselves - or rather, *convince* ourselves - that who, what, where, and how we are is pre-written and set in stone? Damn the script and damn the stones!

In chemistry, if two separate substances are introduced and react, they are transformed permanently. If a person got frostbite and made a seemingly full recovery, you can't let others gaslight you into saying it never happened. Your body holds experiential memories of the life you've endured. Some damage exists below the surface, making typical life tender or sensitive. Memories are the same. One may forget Batman, but a lingering memory exists if prompted well enough.

A trauma coach once described to me that trauma is defined as *any* event that changes our chemistry. Trauma has a generically negative connotation, like the word 'consequences.' To get it out of the way nice and early so there is no pissing contest for whose trauma is worse (or even real, for that matter), let's validate that any event that had any measure of transforming effect on our livelihood is considered trauma. No spectrum of comparing pain and sorrows to others' experiences is necessary.

Even if the matured version of you today could rationalize and bring logic to situations that brought anxiety and panic, we are all susceptible to crumbling under familiar pressures that once overwhelmed us. There is a wounded inner child who can require reassurance that the world is no longer as terrifying as it once was. What is trivial to some can be monumental to others. Very few people will truly know the circumstances that normalized our perception of how this world works. But the good thing is that our sense of 'normalcy' is very flexible.

Anybody, in any experience, can alter our way of being in one day, hour, or moment. If we can find or be offered a perspective that serves our experience better, we need nothing but concentrated effort to shift the entire trajectory. I once met a grown man complaining his leg would cramp while squatting to wipe his bum. He never pondered that he could lean to the side rather than squat. This isn't the same as trauma, but we laugh about how one humorous conversation saved him a lifetime of legwork above the toilet.

There are more effortless ways to go about your life outside your sense of 'normal' perspective. You cannot change what you refuse to speak about. Often, we are so convinced that our 'normal' is entirely acceptable until somebody looks at us with utter shock at our normalized way of being.

Trauma and grief are not facts. They are stories with a beginning, middle, and end. It is only a crisis of healing if we are stuck without knowing how to move forward or having the humility to try. There is an ease and lightness of life waiting for you to experience as you gather the courage to unravel the unspeakable and supposed unchangeable. We are only as sick as our secrets.

No road to recovery or rewiring the serenity of our experience is promised to be smooth. But even smashing through waves head-on is less threatening than pretending it's not coming and being struck from a vulnerable angle.

Bridge Building

I've spent a few years fairly obsessed with understanding consciousness. What's the point if it's not simply *for* us? Why does it haunt us so? Why does it argue with us? And who is the 'me' that is being argued with? Which voices are fueling my earthly desires of survival and sex? And which are the still and quiet whispers of something the world has never seen embodying itself inside of me? How do I separate them? How do I trust the intrusive thoughts are not just an accumulation of sorrows tweaking out and intending to add to the unsteadiness I already feel?

The questions you must ask to enter that discovery space are absolutely maddening. Dare I say, as it *should* be.

"Why *should* it be maddening?" You ask.

Because that god-particle of consciousness is the divine chaos that interrupts us from being nothing but an accumulation of cause-and-effect, consciousness *is* the freedom particle. The freer you realize you are, the more unfathomable power you realize you have in this life.

The DNA of a tree will always be doing tree stuff. It can wind up poles and grow around bicycle frames, but it's still a tree doing tree stuff. We are similar in that when it breaks through as a seed, it does nothing but cater to its maximum potential, flaws and all. What consciousness means for *us* is that I am not just Remmy Stourac. I am everything Remmy Stourac has become up until this point, and then whatever the fuck I want to be. I cannot alter my biology, but I can alter my character, my experience and my fate.

I can surrender my entire experience up to this point if I believe a new lifestyle before me will better serve me and my sense of justice. It's in my ability to weave my intelligence into the potential of anything and everything else.

My thesis on our consciousness (up to this moment) is this: You - All your experiences, emotions, and normalcy have designed a creature of habit. Your consciousness is the bridge that builds your relationship with you, your life, and eternity. Your body and the language that comes with it is the millions of years of ancestor's stories unravelling the beautiful creature you are. It has a loud voice with many deep roots and an ego tied to a sense of worth and place in its surroundings. I believe our consciousness craves harmony because we are fundamentally the fusion of endless generations of collaborated human essence. For better or worse, we are made *of* one another and *for* one another.

If learning something forges a synapse in your mind, then here is where my bridge analogy comes in. If you never heard a guitar before, that is the first synapse, like a rickety board reaching a new island of knowledge. Once you hear multiple songs, your understanding of that instrument grows as a tiny island from which your mind receives information. There is one-way traffic from that island to your mind as you receive its experience.

But the day you pick up the guitar and play it yourself, you start sending traffic to the mental island. You get feedback from the traffic you send to that island and refine your connection to that island of potential. Learning music theory, scales, and strumming patterns expands the bridge and its security in your mind. Eventually, it can become a super-highway with such deep structure and flow that you can play on autopilot. You genuinely fuse yourself with that object's potential.

The same goes for driving a vehicle. Your sense of space is not your body but the entire structure. You learn to drift and weave between obstacles since your consciousness is fused with the dimensions and power of your vehicle. The more it is practiced, the deeper and more fluent the understanding. Most people only drive to work and never learn to drift, so they only build their bridge to a certain understanding. In addition, the bridge of skill to drive and the bridge to maintain a vehicle are two separate islands of knowledge.

This helps explain how we are barraged with information, and islands of products and propaganda are vying to build bridges in our minds. If we aren't diligent, forces can build entire bridges in our consciousness without us really knowing or agreeing to them. It just pelts us with consistent marketing or influence, and we cannot avoid it. So, most of our understanding of the world was bestowed upon us against our will. It's not until we get radically curious about why we think as we do and if we really are rooted in our belief systems. Were we just expected to inherit belief systems and never stress-test them ourselves?

This is how we can build bridges of belief in our minds and be entirely convinced of their validity. Just because the traffic is grandfathered down from generations does not mean it is the best belief system. It just means it is one of countless options of belief. Some islands will contradict and be at war. Some bridges must be torn down and abandoned to harmonize with new belief structures.

You have a certain amount of mental traffic available every day. That mental traffic wanders and daydreams toward different mental islands whether we are aware of it or not. Actively choosing where that traffic goes is how we nurture our identity.

When dropping a habit, it is easier to burn the figurative bridge down, such as blocking an ex-lover's contact, rather than to try to avoid an easily accessible bridge. If a mental island is not good for you, take the necessary measures to make it difficult to use. Just like we take routine paths home, so does our mental traffic. We must rewire our mental roadways to heal faster and shift habits more easily.

It may feel like you are being torn down and rebuilt. That is the functional experience of a piece of identity dying so something better can be built in its place.

On the positive end, you can complementarily take on responsibilities when building relationships. You are not just building one bridge to a person; you are building a bridge to their entire network of wisdom, skills, and assets. Networking is the ultimate life hack to expanding and speeding up the actualization of our potential.

We most easily build those networks through how we actualize our emotions—e-motion—energy in motion. If we can get playful and curious about emotions as a tool rather than just something to receive from how the world affects us, we can live truly free.

Emotional Architecture

Consciousness is also the inescapable narrator that haunts and puppeteers our journey through time and our relationship to that journey. Our journey and our relationship to it are two separate things.

The journey might say I am on my free-willed way to be an author, lawyer, batman, or whatever. My relationship with that journey is my sense of joy or resentment in pursuing that goal or living that lifestyle. I must decide how worthwhile it is to myself, my surroundings, and eternity.

We dance with eternity a lot more than we realize. Imagine any young couple carving their initials into a tree or bench to claim, 'We were here.' But perhaps more deeply, 'This timestamp is a dare to outlast time itself. That love is worth carving into the world in case others forget.'

Romantic and poetic, sure. But with no shortage of delusion, as we all know. I said consciousness is divinely chaotic. Not divinely calculated. I could argue that everything *we* call 'chaos' is divinely ordered as it is entirely outside our will. If you have any inkling of a God narrating the well-being of our life, then everything we see before us is exactly as it is meant to be. Only we have a clear sense of choice and audacity to influence any or all of it.

Kid logic made Batman seem better than cowboys. But my brother had to be a terrible Batman before he realized he was a natural cowboy. Curiosity satisfied. The divine chaos can rest easy. For now, anyway.

The terrifying price of freedom is that the cost of one thing is to abandon all other choices. To 'decide' literally means 'to cut off' or 'to kill', as the Latin origin suggests.

How often do we shun the story of a young adult who tries telling their parents that they are dropping out of college to follow their dreams? They get emotionally and mentally crucified for trying to follow their own intuition. Sure, the consequences are different and more advanced, but so are we. We are built to handle it.

Will we follow the divine chaos that is uniquely given to us? What is the alternative? Why do we crumble under the expectations of other people equally flawed, unsure, and terrified as us? Our power is to rewrite the story in ways that it's never been written before. Is that not mystifying, chilling, and sexy all at once? It's fucking empowering. Now, we need some calculated audacity to follow through.

Our biggest obstacle? Our traumas, grief, and fear. Moments that wove a debilitating sense of dread, sorrow, and anxiety into our experience. With such moments of ecstasy that this life can offer, complimentary horrors were born to bring life to the balance.

Fear not. Grief is but an opportunity to pry open our spirit. If there is one absolute thing I swear to be true, it is that magic can be found in our darkest days.

The Hydra

It wasn't until I wrote this book that I met my father in a newfound light. While pondering various forms of anger, I was curious about our nature to spite God in troubling times. I imagined being in my parents' shoes with having four children, thin finances, and having a youngest child (me) being diagnosed with Leukemia.

I understood what my mom handled as she was constantly with me, whereas my father held down the fort and the well-being of all three other siblings. Having endured what I did, if I were in my father's shoes, I imagine my composure at *least* cracking in a conversation with my creator. I admit I would surely falter, so I wanted to hear straight from my father about how human he was.

After a handful of years retired from his service with the Royal Canadian Mounted Police, he began to relax into a demeanour that wasn't constantly on guard. We started hearing stories that left our jaws on the floor for the near-death experiences he escaped on a typical basis. It humanized him in a way I could never before muster. I wondered why he had such little energy to play and stuck to his solitude when he was home. I know there is plenty he still doesn't care to talk about. I even tried to butter him up by admitting I wouldn't be able to keep my cool if my son was diagnosed with cancer so young. But this is what he said:

"Honestly, I wasn't mad at God." He started.

"Are you *serious*?" I sprung to doubting that claim.

"I remember asking my dad about things he went through in World War 2." He began, "The things he said felt impossible to get through, but he did. I didn't think I could say the same of myself to be as strong if the same hardships happened.

"But when it came to you getting sick, I had been called to enough tragedies at work that I believed I could see the brighter side of you being sick… Did you know I had a nickname at work?"

"No… What nickname?"

"They called me Doctor Death." I could hear him half smiling over the phone at how insane that sounded.

"Get out of here… Doctor *Death*?" I thought he was bluffing.

"In my first few years in the force, I was called to the most homicides, suicides, and fatalities than any other officer in the province. By almost double."

"Holy shit." I pause to let him continue.

"Other officers didn't want to work with me because I was bad luck and got the worst calls. But I had seen enough families come together or make the most of sudden tragedies that I believed we would be ok. Even if you were going to be taken from us too soon, I knew, or at least I would find a way that we would be ok. Because we would have to be."

"So, you're telling me that we come from a long line of unlucky men who are just... built for it?" I'm still in shock at the nickname.

"What other choice do we have?"

He had a point. He told me stories I couldn't write here without doubling this book into the horror genre. I was dumbstruck for days on end by the things I had no idea he endured. I had a moment of self-pity to consider the grief we gave him for not playing with us as kids or being such a hard ass. It's a miracle he even made it home some days.

On the other hand, how should a spouse or children understand and step up to fill a gap that comes from a reason so foul that it cannot be spoken of? Not all grief is made equal, but it can be suppressed, buried, and embodied in such a way that those we love are caught in the crossfire.

The things we've spent a lifetime stuffing away or pretending aren't affecting us follow us. How we compensate grows new heads of the hydra. Drugs, alcohol, gambling, rage, depression, lying... all the countless ways we escape the weight of the hand we've been dealt. Even if we cut off one head that exists as a symptom of the suffering, it can grow another ugly head if it is not healing the core of the grief itself.

In a lifestyle like being a first responder, it is not exactly possible to eliminate exposure to grief and trauma. Our two options are building resilience to the stress and surrounding ourselves with as much love and support as possible. If that negative energy does not have a healthy way to be processed, redirected and unburdened, it's no surprise it is stored and manifests in painful ways.

Grief is a Passage

As said above, grief is a story with a beginning, middle and end. Depression is not a characteristic but a healing crisis. It is a story that simply does not know how to unfold further. Yet!

Is it fair to say that a negative emotion would not stay if you had the power to overcome it? Envy would be a brief feeling if you knew how to quickly and ethically acquire your own richness, right? Anger would only be a brief indicator of a lack of harmony. You would act and re-harmonize the environment. Negative emotions stagnate and build in the body when there is a sense of powerlessness.

All negative emotions are learned in relation to our powerlessness—not intentionally, but in response to our sense of injustice and our inability to correct it. Just like we cannot correct a loved one's sudden death by bringing them back to life, we can only redirect and maximize our love elsewhere in their absence. Justice does not always take obvious forms. Otherwise, we would act towards it more often.

Insecurity, inadequacy, fear, and hate are learned. Envy, jealousy, selfishness, pride… they're all learned in relation to our sense of capability to right what we consider to be wrong. It's our emotional relationship with our own place in the world and what we consider justice in how it unfolds.

These emotions are all in relation to our belief system of *what is, what it ought to be, and how we can make it so*. We remain powerful if we have a realistic map between what is and what could be.

All pain is simply some form of separation from our personal reality and our idea of its harmony. Separation from love, sense of self, sense of reality, physical health, etc., It is an interesting mental, emotional, and spiritual exercise to consider pain in relativity to a level of separation. It suggests how deeply our sense of *attachment* plays in every situation.

We have a wildly undervalued capacity to slow down our reactions to life's troubles. If we are curious about our attachment to the circumstance, we can give ourselves time to properly evaluate the more appropriate response. Our initial emotion is rarely the most productive response. The more distance you can make between reacting and intelligently responding, your sense of power over feelings will grow.

The involuntary grievance unveils how we truly felt in relation to what we have been separated from. Perhaps this is why it is said that *discipline is self-love in motion*. We can reorganize our reality if we have the courage to approach and study our grief rather than run from it. We can reorganize our attachments within life and find a way to prosper spiritually, mentally, and emotionally off what would otherwise be our downfall.

Whatever wages war on our personal sense of *what ought to be* and *how we can make it so* can cause us incredible grievances. But if we can cultivate the discipline to recalibrate our attachments to the world's ever-changing ways, we may bend, but we will not be broken so long as we live.

I thoroughly stand by the summary that grief embodies unspent love that can't find a place to go. I approach this subject with utmost caution and respect, as any reader who crosses these words could carry an unspeakable grievance. I do not intend in any thought to belittle the weight or immensity of a sorrow. But I *do* wish to inspire our sense of triumph and transformation despite these woes. I could never captivate a grand spectrum of grief in just one chapter, though there is a frame of mind to go on the divine offensive against grief.

There is vital information hidden in our grievances that sheds light on our soul in a way that no other sensation can.

Grief can freeze our psyches in time to a moment of devastation. There is something we consider proper about the mourning to be had and the flag we fly to claim, 'The world is lesser-so for having lost you.' This statement - as true as it may be - capitalizes the sorrow in a way that may prolong it. Instead, saying, 'The world was enriched for the time we shared with you' is a minor but monumental tweak. Would you rather emphasize your favourite memories? Or have them orbit in pale comparison to your grief of losing them? Grief may bring us to our knees, but I dare say it is the demand to celebrate goodness as we had it. The ultimate honour of a good thing is to pay forward that love to others in tribute to the lost love we feel.

The world can sometimes feel a shortage of goodness - if not most times. But there is nothing to win in claiming that the goodness is dwindling when you and I are still here to carry it out. We are still here; it is enough because it has to be.

Grief is embodied in nearly every negative side effect the body can muster: Physical, mental, emotional, and even spiritual pain. Everybody's equilibrium is shaken differently for a season or sometimes even a lifetime. In a big world, grand battles are fought with bullets, bombs, or mere words. To speak courage, love and truth into a life after grief is no trivial act. When grief is external, we call upon gratitude. When grief brews internally, we call upon grace.

I Could Make a Difference

Sharing perspective and opening to one another can help us re-calibrate reality when it feels impossible to do alone. We can be so deeply embedded in our ways that it could *only* take the grace, love, and patience of another to shift our reality to harmony again. When we stop growing and evolving, we feel like we are rotting from within. This can soon manifest outwardly in our lives in ways we escape and mask our pain. When the path between what life is and how it ought to be feels impossible to achieve, we lose hope. Let me paint this picture with one of my own closest calls with self-destruction.

After thirteen months of writing my first fantasy novel, *The Reaper's Inception*, I was savagely humbled by how the universe actually works. I put my whole life's savings into professionally assisted self-publishing that book. I assumed sheer faith in my own capacity to tell a fantastical story, and my servitude to donate 10% of proceeds to Kid's Cancer Care would compensate me generously. My inexperienced mind was high on possibility and had no roots in reality. Just because something is available to the whole world doesn't mean it sells itself.

I went as far as to guesstimate my first month's revenue and bought a Costco shopping cart full of candy for an upcoming Halloween teen weekend at Kids Cancer Care Camp. I felt generous with a few hundred dollars and didn't care if it was more than 10%. That mountain of candy I got was *forty* times more expensive than my first-quarterly book revenue. All the colour left my face. My reality crumbled when I realized what position I put myself in.

Having put my whole life's savings into publishing and being totally delusional about the fact that no marketing meant no money, I now had a financial crisis. I went from well and comfy to borrowing money from my parents to pay rent. My self-righteous attempt to pay it forward and sacrifice a year of creativity landed me in absolute turmoil. All my money fears overwhelmed me, convincing me that my inability to execute my grand vision made me unstable.

I spiralled for days and weeks, pushing people I loved away. I entirely lost hope that my ambitions had any realistic basis to support anymore. It became an entire identity crisis that I would have to resort to recalibrating my life and downgrade myself as a visionary. I kneecapped my self-respect and positioned myself to convince my current girlfriend that I wasn't worth dating. I tried to convince her that I was a sinking ship worth avoiding for her own good. I remember being in the fetal position in my bed, midday, trying to break up with her over text and throw a year-and-a-half of the best relationship I ever had away. A quarter-life crisis at the ripe age of 21.

She convinced me to drive to her to talk in person despite me being entirely committed to breaking up with her as the *selfless* thing to do. She usually had a graceful approach but got mad enough to give me the tough love that shattered my illusions of inadequacy. She gave me one of the most significant memories of grace in my young life.

"What is this really about?" She prodded.

After a lot of dancing around the answer I finally managed, "I'm shit scared that if what I pitch as my life's calling makes me feel like such an incompetent loser when my best effort leaves me broke. How am I supposed to give you any peace that I can take care of you? My ambitions are clearly delusional. I think paying a big enough price and being a good enough person will magically have the universe slap back with abundance."

She outright refused to let me break up with her and told me this was not where my story ended. She told me that just because my dream crumbled, I was no less deserving of love. It was the first time I shattered into tears in my adult life. In an upbringing that told me crying made me pathetic, she held me and said, "This is the strongest thing I've ever seen you do."

That *wrecked* me. I thought she was full of shit and that this wasn't what being strong looked like. Yet I remained there quaking as she held me. My reality *of what is, what could be, and how I could make it so* had to be entirely rewritten. But I was no lesser of a man to have to start over.

But I was not starting over. I was starting from experience.

As my delusion and grief crippled my sense of self, she was able to lend me hope and confidence. Being open to show how much pain I was really in allowed me to take the first step to not staying that way. She had a vision for me that was greater than what I could offer myself. From that day forward, I understood how vulnerability was not only a strength, but it was also an absolute necessity to be seen, understood and truly loved. Such profound sorrows and fears can only be fought with equally audacious grace and love. Her relentless confidence in me was better than anything I could offer myself. This was the bridge to recovering my serenity that I may not have ever found without such a profound moment of surrender.

The story of transformation keeps us *alive*! We pay to see it, read it, play through it in video games, and have others tell us we can do it. So, what's holding us back?

Fear. Fear is the basis that no matter what our foundational perspectives of reality are, we are not enough to bring it to fruition. Even if we fail, failure is not final. It is only as fatal as we allow it to be.

Love has made poets of us all. Poetry is the special intensity that is given to the expression of a feeling or idea. The act of love is how we add beauty to the world. It does not matter objectively if something is ugly. Treating it with love is bringing beauty into the world by instilling value somewhere it wasn't before. In a world where grief would harden us into allowing unforgivable atrocities to swallow all the beauty in the world, love will save us all.

Call that corny, but this is a war as deep and dirty as heaven and hell on earth. We need each other and our unique distortion of the world to shake each other back to see the world in a bearable way to continue. To maximize what we were made for. The fear of reaching out for help in this crazy world may be one of the silliest fears we've ever had. We need to be mad enough to make a difference and admit the weight of the world can be too much to bear.

Like my father said, "We are built for it."

Fate and Freedom

So, there is fate... and there is freedom. For this exact moment, I believe them to be in opposition. Yet simultaneously, they are two forces always reaching out to each other. If freedom is the arrow we shoot, fate is the entire target on which we land. A bullseye would be the perfect form of acquiring every detail of our goal, whereas the rest of the target is everything that comes as a byproduct of our freedom.

The more audacious our goals, the more unpredictable all those possible byproducts that chaos can weave into our future. It is within us to take all that chaos and order it to our own harmony. Sometimes, that means a decade-long dream alongside somebody must end if the discontent outweighs the harmony. To re-order our path, we take everything good and prosperous about what we've experienced and use that material to build bridges to better days.

Internal grief can manifest when we have created a bullseye target that is impossible to hit. Nobody else can see this imaginary target of desire that cannot match our fantasy to reality. Its the same mental work of the three perspectives, yet sometimes our outlandish desires have us totally detached from the imperfections that come with real life. If we cannot adore and make peace with imperfections, we will be the maker of our own constant grief.

Self-created grief is consistently failing at your ideal of 'this goal' by 'this timeline.' That's it. Rearrange your goal and timeline to something you can sustainably accomplish each day, and the joy of the journey will sustain you.

Harmony can be mental and emotional flexibility with our ambitions while reality shifts and challenges us. If we refuse to take inventory of reality and the consequences of how we show up for it, we become a victim of fate. This is how we assume freedom and harmony have escaped us. Freedom is greater than fate in this ideal:

If we can supersede our reactions and become creatures of purpose and intelligent response, we can truly die having chosen our own fates.

Even if we, the arrow, are intercepted and turned into shrapnel mid-flight, we at least die while flying. Having never strived is no life at all.

Whether you want to be Batman or a cowboy, show up relentlessly and unapologetically to the life you deem worth fighting for. And when it feels like hell, I hope you have the humility to re-calibrate your reality. Asking for help might be the strongest move you'll ever make.

Chapter 9

Humanity 101

Every morning, you wake up as the inheritor of yesterday's effort. Imagine you get a body swap with your best friend or a loved one. If you could have them wake up and be overwhelmingly grateful for what you accomplished on their behalf in a day, what would you have done for them?

Now, the trick question is this: Why do we not act like that best friend visiting our own body every day? If we wanted our best friend to lose some excess weight or experience sobriety, imagine we could spend one day in their body eating the right food and refraining from substances so they could wake up with more energy the next day. We can wake up and thank ourselves for yesterday's work.

Let's get real; we would all peak at our friend or loved one's bank account and consider what borderlines the acceptable measure of recklessness. It's just one day of body-swapping, right? Why not maximize pleasure, knowing the mess and feelings will have to be cleaned up by whoever wakes up in that body tomorrow? That's *tomorrow-you's* problem.

That seems to be how we act about ourselves, isn't it? I'll self-soothe and coast through today by as comfortable methods as possible. I'm sure that future me is the badass who will make up for the deficits I feel today.

That's what debt means. We constantly bargain with the future and don't realize it. We have depersonalized the future like we have depersonalized and discredited our past. Or at least we discredit it in a way that suggests our future self wasn't worth buying into. Guess who landed you in the body and mindset you have today? The person who forgot that they were their own best friend.

For you personally, what would make up the qualities of a best friend? Consider that question to the most elaborate depth you can offer. Then, go *be* that person for others in the world.

I'm dead serious, just like the gratitude list. Don't keep reading until you've pondered that to a satisfying answer.

Befriending Yourself

Imagine you again got that chance to body-swap with somebody you cared about. They have been confiding in you that they've been terrified to apply for that dream job, ask for that guy or girl's number or invest in themselves. You would have that opportunity to do the groundwork on their behalf, so the thing they fantasize about could be in actual motion by the following day. Even if it's not promised to work, it's better than a dead-end fantasy in which its only function is currently making you feel unworthy. Your fantasies and daydreams are supposed to empower you.

You are on duty as that best friend for yourself, too. You can't pass off that courage or fear to somebody else. As much as you'd like to, even if possible, there is an inkling that having somebody else do it would cheat you of the true experience, right? Would you genuinely believe somebody deserved that guy or girl's number if they could not even ask for it? Why would any dream job be seeking fearful people? They wouldn't. Something of value is magnetizing for a reason. We shape our sense of self-worth to rise to the occasion despite our feelings. That's true willpower.

The alternative is being the adversary in your own body. (I will dive deeper into this adversarial quality in the 'Manage the Monster' chapter.) It's like body-swapping into your loved one's body and procrastinating so long that their intuition and inspiration is stifled. You'll learn to ignore intuition towards genuine enthusiasm. Why offer excitement if you're not going to pursue it anyway?

The ways we justify procrastination are sinister. Perhaps you front a lofty, unfathomable goal and give yourself anxiety at its magnitude rather than offer yourself bite-sized chunks to start. Perhaps you start a relational argument to create something seemingly important to steal your focus from what you should really do.

In the worst case of self-sabotage, we allow ourselves to sit and be endlessly pleasured by less meaningful activities than the thing that beckons us. We can't self-soothe ourselves into a bold new experience.

The adventure demands play outside of the comfort zone. Nobody can do it for you. But like a best friend, you can do the hard things for who will inherit your experience tomorrow.

The Forever-Wars

Many people barely feel above the water in their well-being. So, let's dial it back and momentarily take away the bigger ambitions. Let's say you entered that loved one's body for a day and realized their house is a bit of a mess. They have neglected taxes to organize, weeds in the yard, a dentist appointment to schedule, etc. The list could be endless. Some micro-tasks will always be stacking up and becoming subconscious proof that there are things not tended to. I'll say this often: The most sinister thing about our excuses is that we validate them.

I think most of us have been distraught when we mature from being dependent to independent and realize how ill-equipped we are with essential life skills. Most of us aren't taught how to maintain a vehicle, no basic building skills, homecare, self-care, emotional regulation, bartering, negotiation, healthy communication, and so on. You'd think one of the most fundamental lessons in life would be work/life balance, financial literacy, healthy coping mechanisms and relationship maintenance. Most people are pretending they aren't barely above emotional drowning.

If you could be that friend who body-swaps into somebody's life and tends to the mundane, annoying tasks we all must face, then something cool happens. That person will have to look around them, see that things are well and in order, and decide whether to play or build in that truly satiated state. That person will bargain with investing in their future self or perpetuate the endless play and maintenance lifestyle. If you change nothing, you obviously get the same life today as you do twenty years from now. That's your bargain. But the forever-war of daily maintenance and lifestyle struggles will sustain. If you don't courageously impose yourself into a different future, you have no right to complain that you've misused your well-being.

Trying is a spiritual experience. You are building a relationship with potential itself. If you don't try, then no kidding; you have no relationship with your potential. You do not need faith inside your safety net. But you do have to summon courage and a worthwhile reason to be a part of the human symphony on bravery.

Lucky are those who feel guilt. This foul feeling proves that an internal compass exists. It allows us to reconcile and correct ourselves. If there is no sense of injustice to our own potential and harmony, then we will be shocked when years pass and we have little to be proud of.

We were literally brought into this world through orgasmic pleasure. Just as I've expressed that love is the opposite of fear, I mean it like this: If fear is self-preservation, then the opposite – love

– must be others-amplifying. Love is leaving yourself and others better than you found them. If you don't tend to yourself to have an overflow, then no kidding, it feels impossible to take on more than you're not already handling well.

The essence and creation of life itself is orgasmic pleasure. To love is to inject your enthusiasm and passion into existence. The sheer influence of those ecstatic expressions will enrich others. Whether it be joining you or simply witnessing your full expression, the collective is empowered as a reminder of what we are made of. You can't expect that ultimate expression to manifest in yourself if you are procrastinating and defeated by trivial tasks.

Base-Level Harmony

If you're left feeling incapable and overwhelmed by the mandatory tasks of daily upkeep, you will not have much to offer more large-scale battles. Whether you believe society has intentionally educated us directionally against our fullest actualization as individuals or not, we have significant and obvious gaps in our communal welfare. Wherever you see a gap in well-being, we can be of service. Becoming exceptional in merely one line of human health, fitness, regulation, or conflict resolution is an overwhelming victory for the collective.

Confident, stable, and secure people typically start making decisions and lifestyle moves that are bigger than themselves. They are difference-makers because they have their own situation covered, so thinking bigger is the logical next step. If they can't accomplish the next goal alone, then bringing others into a stable excess is a valiant task.

Sadly, there is this strange cushy societal net that keeps us in the limbo of not thriving but not exactly fully suffering. This makes us slowly deteriorate with a lack of meaning rather than having a clear cause and effect of why we are where we are. This makes it seem self-inflicted. Instead, we lack basic development that should be ground zero education for everybody.

Especially EQ. Emotional quotient, or emotional intelligence. When our playground of life becomes bigger than ourselves and we can harmonize with others, we need to know healthy communication and conflict resolution. Our ability to self-regulate and have integrity transpires over how realistic we can harmonize with others. Only when two or more people can be entirely independent and conspire together can we create 'We' problems. If we are insecure and constantly competing for gain or recognition, we can never surpass 'You vs. Me' problems.

Anything from simple cleanliness issues between roommates like, "Hey, do you mind cleaning up in the kitchen fully when you're done so I'm not cleaning up after you? I appreciate your diligence." Everybody has different standards. But asking for harmony is not wrong or immoral. The benefit of the doubt in others' willingness to do good plays a major role in that going smoothly.

If you can't have uncomfortable conversations, your whole life becomes uncomfortable.

The energetic and emotional tension beats on you if you don't beat through the tension. Then a simple problem is too far gone, and then we start calling each other bitches and assholes when our real desire is harmony. So, instead, we've emotionally and intellectually beat each other into submission? That's the dumbest (most inefficient) route we can take. How is that the typical tactic most people find themselves using?

We need a more compelling reason 'why' to strengthen the harmonious whole. Because other people make up most of our life experience. Yes, we need to learn how to count, but I bet kids would be more invested if we told them our entire lifestyle depends on their financial literacy. Yeah, we need to learn to write, but if we told kids that words are the weapons that we will fight every meaningful argument in our life with, then it's dumb *not* to read and become literately powerful. Instead, we bicker over chump change because we are broke and call each other 'pricks' when emotions take over and we don't know how to express our desired harmony.

Our 'injustice' conditioning reacts faster than our logic catches up. Partially because I think we as humans understand how pathetic our issues are. That is what summons abrupt bursts of rage. We have a decade of education and are supposed to break the surface of society as blooming plants, ushering in a new era of abundance. Instead, we are pissed off because we can barely regulate our needs, ask for help, or fend for ourselves without being embarrassed that we don't know better by now.

The Walking Wounded

No single person on earth gets through life without joining the rest of us as the 'walking wounded.' Our wounds shape us just as much as the healing does. But the wounds should never outweigh our desire to heal. Otherwise, we recycle our trauma-induced character traits as victims because…?

Because *why*?

Because healing is harder than staying wounded the rest of our lives? What backward-ass logic is that? You didn't ask for your pain, but it is your personal burden for the rest of your life, regardless. The only thing that could keep us attached to pain would be our egos trying to preserve our identity of not being as insecure as we feel. But, when met with compassion, grace, and love, we allow people to know they are no lesser-than for having been wounded by the world.

We are allowed to be pissed off and still use love, grace, and compassion as the solution. I'm pissed off that there are generations of heroes suffering their own heroics for us and being outcasted and belittled for enduring wickedness *on our behalf*. But yelling at other people and professionals to help them won't change this story. It takes *me*. It takes *you*.

It takes *us* meeting the wounded where they are and embracing them in a way that they know they are more than their wounds. We must have each other's backs in the ugly fight it will take to rehabilitate the suffering out of our spirits. We can't fight another's battle for them, but it costs us nothing to speak life into the downtrodden. Our love is the great reducer of ego. This fucking magical idea of love calls upon something beyond us that defines us as less separate from one another.

I'm not trying to narrow our efforts to the unsung heroes. Some of us are born with addictions thanks to our parents' best efforts to escape their suffering. Wounds on every level can be shattered with unshakable grace. It doesn't matter who or where we have been. Our whole life story is defined by what's next. It's what we wake up for, even if we don't know that. We can be in soul-sucking monotony for decades and live on that one hope.

Every ounce of suffering ever considered has been outplayed by the idea that tomorrow is a new story. Our compassion for one another is the mental first aid that helps stifle the emotional bleeding. This compassion shows that we are bigger than what we try to outrun. This is not for the faint of heart.

We are allowed to be pissed off at the idea that people believe their past dictates their future. We are allowed to be pissed off that people lack faith that this pain we endure is all there is to it, and there is nothing better around the bend. We are allowed to be pissed off that people feel so alone that they believe another's faith in them is a waste of time because they have a history of letting loved ones down. We are allowed to be pissed off that countless generations endured all of their bullshit, and we have the audacity not to want to see the next day through? We are the product of way too many of our ancestors having faith in tomorrow for us to be the ones who lost hope. The fire we feel from all the injustice can be geared toward sharpening one another. To be emboldened not to flinch when somebody confides in us and needs a spiritual place to rest.

I wage this war with grace, unconditional love, and compassion. Because your battle is my battle. I didn't ask for this life, and you didn't ask for yours. In that, we are not separate.

Take note of every gap in well-being you see in the world for one week. The amount of opportunities you will see as soon as you look may astound you. Being of service to one another is what makes our home worth fighting for. It would be my greatest delight to be of any fragment of a reason that keeps you here. May we perpetuate hope that tomorrow's surprises can justify all the difficulty we have endured.

We can be that surprise for one another. Show up daily like a best friend to yourself and humanity. You'll be amazed how it will inevitably respond in kind.

Chapter 10

Right Next Door

Did you know that when people go off to war, it is critical to convince soldiers they are fighting some form of evil? Calling an enemy evil sounds obvious, but they don't hand out personal profiles of enemy soldiers because it would only take a few minutes to notice they aren't much different than us. You aren't going overseas to potentially kill fathers, mothers, friends, sons and daughters. You're going to destroy evil. Even if it can finally be rationalized to be 'the right thing to do,' we decide the force of evil has gone beyond control or redemption, and we will be the hand that smites it.

Dehumanizing the opposition carries many benefits, though we are also dehumanized through the act. Some benefits provide moral clarity and group cohesion in both shared purpose and minimized doubt. The problem with such propaganda is that it fails to foster peace, and the momentum of violence has passed down through our generations. It is a momentum of violence built on the perspective of necessity.

When gears shift, and there is an effort of harmony, moral injuries, trauma, and guilt are revealed in the journey to reconcile. Every emotion and action has momentum. It is either violence and fear or the attempt of harmony and love for one another as a nation.

I heard a psychological trick: if a stranger is getting frustrated with you and coming in hot, introduce yourself and try to shake their hand (or some gesture of goodwill) as fast as possible. It's easy to be mad at an anonymous stranger who wronged you, but learning names breaks the veil of anonymity. It's not a magic fixer but a start to humanizing a problem. We think somebody is just being careless if we get in a minor fender-bender until they say, "Hi, I'm Amy… Sorry, my husband just passed. I haven't slept, and my baby is sick; I've been making a lot of mistakes lately."

The energy just shifted, didn't it? Suddenly the context of the incident makes us re-evaluate our attitude. Now, that anonymous problem became an exhausted grieving mother. It's pretty hard to stay angry when we get even the slightest glimpse of somebody else's current suffering and its momentum. We might even feel compelled to understand that if not you, somebody else less graceful could be in the crossfire, and you have an opportunity to console her. Maybe we really show up for the moment and take that grieving mother grocery shopping to turn compounding difficulty into a serendipitous moment.

We can change the tides of misfortune with the conscious momentum of selfless servitude. Being wronged does not justify the perpetuation of wrongdoing and malicious energy. It is not easy or effortless, but we have the power to bring the momentum of pain and grief—even in small instances—to a standstill.

Just Down the Road

I'm very grateful one of my current roommates has used her hard upbringing to create herself as a mentor for troubled youth in our community. She works at a boy's and girl's club and a halfway house, usually coming home with stories of rebellious kids acting out in bizarre ways for attention. My roommate is amazing at being both a friend and a mentor for these kids as she levels with them and hears their stories. It's no surprise that they are having temper tantrums. Their parents are active alcoholics, abusers, heavy drug users or no longer present. Even at their worst, these kids are an upgrade of character from what their parents are modelling.

One of these young girls at the youth shelter is on the verge of turning 18. She always leaves late at night in skimpy outfits and returns with huge wads of cash. The cops have been called so often on her that her 'reported missing' calls are literally turned down from so many repeat attempts to help her. Both of this girl's parents died around the age of 10, and she has been in the custody of government housing ever since. This girl never had a chance of a normal life from the beginning. This is all happening to people within blocks of where I live.

When was the last time somebody else frustrated you, and you first considered, 'How can I serve them?'

If you think somebody disservices you, why would your reaction be to add value to them? The immediate sensation of anger - or desire for justice - must suggest they owe *you*. But have you ever tried making that request a secondary notion after ensuring the offender is doing OK before you vilify them? We all have blind spots. If the person truly turns out to be a jackass in every sense of the word, well, then at least you did your due diligence.

Now in this furthering trouble, you get to practice patience with people who delight in being a problem. The thing about people who like being a problem is that they feel very small in the rest of their lives. Otherwise, they wouldn't feel the need to act so powerfully in trivial times. The easiest picture to paint on this would be people who take time out of their lives to belittle strangers online. Imagine a person's inner turmoil to draw any delight from making others feel small. Thinking like that is as close to a mental disease as it comes.

Again, disease is being broken down to a disruption of harmony. It means it's not just a bunch of microscopic bugs as we portray sickness but anything outside the sensation of peace, clarity, and well-being. Just as a common cold is contagious, so is potentially other's inability to love themselves. How absolutely unattractive it would be if those people just admitted, 'I'm rude to strangers in my spare time because I never learned how to regulate myself. So, I delight in soliciting shame to people who try to express themselves because my expression is stifled.'

Pain must be such a reoccurring theme in people's lives to create a normalcy of acting like that. Our patience, humility, and kindness are the only plausible methods to raising people out of those states. I honestly do not believe it is in lack of opportunity of love, but lack of its presence that people find it so foreign. Deep in my heart, I can only believe grown men anonymously swear at children over video games and don't feel shame because they are projecting their own normalcy on the next generation.

If we see somebody as 'immature,' then we need to give them the grace that they never knew better. But simultaneously, we must have the backbone of boundaries to demand a quality of character if we are to continue experiencing life around them. If we are to carry the burden of elevating others, we must also be capable of protecting the peace that they might dysregulate or threaten.

People do not emotionally shoot themselves in the foot and sign up for a difficult life when they have a clear path to limit their suffering. On the other hand, I *do* believe people without any sense of harmonious purpose will selfishly indulge and abuse power wherever they can. With no direction worthy of striving, the exaggerated emotions to dominate in trivial problems must be where they compensate for an aimless life.

Not a single person is entirely sane. We are all the walking wounded in some emotional, spiritual, physical, and psychological degree. Some hide it better than others. But thinking anybody has it all together and is short on flaws, your delusion is deeper than you realize. Millionaire cries of loneliness, the most serene monk still breaks composure, and the biggest smile quivers when you're not looking.

I Bet...

I went for a late-night walk during a stint of writer's block. It was barely fifteen minutes before I had this epiphany in noticing so many people's houses still lit up well past midnight. I bet every single house I walked past had somebody inside who had to take deep breaths before they arrived at work so nobody noticed the bad news that kept them up all night. I bet everyone has been so sad that their stomach rejects food. I bet every single man and woman has wondered how the hell they got where they are and are torn between being worried and excited about what's next for them. I bet everyone has had cold sweats from eating the wrong food and narrowly made it to the bathroom in time. I bet some of them even shat themselves, but they may never tell you that.

I bet they question the validity of every choice they ever make and ponder an alternate reality where even one or two significant choices could alter the course of everything that happened to them. I bet every single one of them looks in the mirror and occasionally - or frequently - wishes their features were different. I bet none of them realize how much their friends adore and appreciate them because we rarely express that to each other.

I bet they've all had a thought that felt like a million-dollar idea that escaped because they assumed they wouldn't forget it. I bet they've had such outlandish dreams that they wake up wishing the dream never ended. Likewise, having such a profound nightmare and feared ever having to return to sleep. I bet they have their guards up because their kindness has been taken advantage of, yet they crave the connection they are afraid to open to.

I bet they all have habits they wish didn't have so much power over them. I bet they all question their sacrifices when what seems like the right choice bites them in the ass. I bet they've all wondered what their spirit animal was, what God is real, and why it hasn't made itself more obvious. I bet they've had moments where things seemed so dark that even non-believers took a chance at prayer because they had nothing left. I bet they also forgot about thanking fate when things got comfortable again. I bet they all have fears and mistakes they are trying to outrun.

I can guess every single one of these things because I am these people. Except I've been so unbelievably lucky to have not shat myself... yet. I respect irony far too much to state that and not assume the universe will test my humility.

Sonder

But Remmy, some people are just terrible people!

You know what? You're not wrong. Absolutely some people are cruel and emotionless with their choices. Do you know how both heroes and villains have origin stories? That means cause-and-effect matters. Love and hate are learned feelings and conditions. Everybody with a problem should be a teacher or a warrior, right? What's the point of being angry about the conditions of the world if you're not creating yourself as a solution or at least a defender of things worth fighting for? If you choose to do nothing, you will be a victim of the crossfire of other's suffering. Whether compassionate or cruel, all these characters are equally likely to be your neighbours.

Do you live your life in such a manner as to be the neighbour people pray for? Or are you the one who makes others always look over their shoulder because we never made a fond introduction?

Your presence, near or far, creates the entire atmosphere of everybody else's human experience as they pass you.

There is a word, Sonder, which is the idea that everybody lives a life as complex, strange, and full of surprises as your own. All nearly eight billion of the rest of us are the heroes in our own story. We all spend 24/7 in our own heads, and that's exactly as scary and wonderful as you think it sounds.

Did you know that a 2015-2018 study shows approximately 13% of Americans over the age of 12 are on anti-depressants?[ii] That means there is about a one-in-nine chance each person you cross may be artificially suppressing their sorrow. That doesn't include the population who are also suffering but refuse to medicate. Everyone will have at least one significant tragedy that could justify the despair worthy of being subscribed to an anti-depressant. How did we get so disconnected that we could assume most strangers haven't been wrung out with sorrow enough to deserve grace as a default? When in reality, we have a hopelessness epidemic running so rampant that we pass it off as normal.

If you can have faith in one law of the universe, let it be balance. If a balance of positive and negative exists in all experiences, then the foulest pain a human can inflict on one another is equal to the amount of healing and love we can share. I believe we have a choice in which we choose to amplify in the world every day. There is no neutral ground to be had. Everything is always flowing in life, with new beginnings and new endings making space for the next wave of experience.

Trauma interrupts the plot from unfolding. Our trauma response is the defensive position we take as a strategy to avoid revisiting old pains in new opportunities. But life demands to be lived.

The Necessary Curiosity

The most disturbing thing I personally took from studying antidepressants was the negative side effects. Studies found a frequent effect called 'Apathy Syndrome' developing in users. Apathy syndrome involves a loss of motivation, creativity, desire for play and curiosity.[iii] If people lost their curiosity and desire to play as a side effect of manufactured happiness... doesn't that mean curiosity, play, and creativity are the major factors in authentic happiness?

Let me make one very distinct difference. Tragedy and evil are not the same thing. I do not believe there was anything evil about the cancer that nearly took my life as a young child. There is nobody or no root force to blame in that microscopic battle in a child's life that's barely begun. It is no different than a wolf hunting a deer. I was the young buck, and the cancer was a hungry wolf that nearly won if not for the internal chemical warfare the doctors fought on my behalf.

If nature were evil, we would have destroyed it all by now. But no, we study it. We admire it. We relate to it. We are better because of our greater understanding of it. Calling something a tragedy is a personal relationship to an event. The things that nature has designed as seasons of growth, decay, and devastation lay space for its new beginnings. When did we lose touch that we are of nature too?

On the other hand, I will not tackle evil as a whole, but I will tackle the idea of a 'sin.' That seems to be a biblical word, but understanding it has real utility. When it is taken outside its religious box, its most universal understanding is 'to miss the mark.' That suggests there is something proper to aim at that keeps us well and harmonious.

But Remmy, we weren't taught how to pursue what it is to thrive!

I'm right there with you, amigo.

In this distinction of what a sin is, if we aren't yet aware of how to best find something worth aiming at, we learn to discover and play again. The solution is to approach life with child-like curiosity and squeeze every fibre of joy out of each moment in front of us.

If you're committed to sorrow, I have no doubt you will keep it. Even the pursuit of well-being is riddled with confusion, trial and error, personal discovery, and new beginnings—new beginnings that might seem even scarier than the old familiar sorrow we have made home of. One thing that scares me more than anything is that if I carry old bricks into my new life, I will build the same house.

But if you are committed to gratitude, I have no doubt it will sprout beyond your will. If you take one day to look at everything you use but haven't crafted yourself, gratitude in daily awe can begin.

I have not thanked the people who built the roof I sit under. Nor the people who manufactured the mattress I rest each night. I wrote this book with a language I didn't invent. I communicate my experience through music I didn't craft. I feel the daily safety in my community that others have bled for. I've survived because of medical advancements I had no part in discovering.

We are all nothing but mix-and-remastered versions of the communities and normalcies offered by previous human efforts. We are just the trickle-down intelligence of endless ancestors born through literal orgasmic energy. Enthusiasm can be the baseline experience if we only learn how to penetrate the life experience appropriately to our potential.

There are some tasks we think are unfathomably boring, like reading the dictionary. But if it weren't for that incredible weapon, I would not be as capable of communicating my desires and ideas. Somebody had to pay the price of knowing something was unhealthy, poisonous, or dangerous for us to live healthier, safer lives. Somebody had to try all the medicine and suffer the consequences of side effects for us to make intelligible decisions about the risk/reward of substances we try. Strangers have suffered on our behalf every single day since the beginning of time. There is absolutely purpose in pain, but reliving pain that has already been explored on our behalf is not necessary.

The Power in Community

Every person you ever loved was once a stranger. Every person who inspired you was a stranger. Every person who made the movies, games, toys, art, and music you love is a stranger. Yes, the opposite reciprocates just the same with those who broke your heart, left you stranded, and left you unappreciated. But if your commitment to validating old pain strains you from welcoming new friends and experiences around the corner, you choose to let your sorrow narrate a limited life.

That is a sin. Merely living to avoid pain is a monumental miss in aiming for quality and lasting pleasures. Just like playing exclusively defense in every sport means you aren't actively moving towards scoring your own points. You must build the skill set of offensive play to win the game.

It is beyond 'missing the mark' to not only miss a goal but never to create one besides avoiding pain. That is merely surviving. Rather, crafting a meaningful direction and justifying your pain in pursuit of it changes *everything*. You'll experience pain regardless, but you can have a better relationship with it. Hiding your gifts is an insult to your intelligence. Being closed off to the goodness hiding in every day is a sin.

Strangers will make up the majority of the way you experience this journey. Everybody, at all times, is teaching each other how to be human. If you aren't sure how you'd like to be, you will be caught in the waves of other's influence until you harness your character and strategize your influence. We can envision the future and make it all possible by understanding patterns and past experiences to build expectations of the future. Remember that? *What is, what ought to be, and how we can make it so.*

At the end of the day, you don't know what you don't know. So I repeat: If you carry old bricks to your new home, you build the same house. The spice of life is behind everything you haven't yet experienced. New friends crack open new worlds we never knew existed. That is how much richness can hide behind every face we somehow forget to admire as a hero writing their own story. If you can learn to romanticize the curiosity of life again, you will see its beauty hiding inside everything you don't yet understand. Behind every assumption, you walk shallowly in a world of rich depth. You will miss the vastness of every stranger's story.

The intense anticipation of imagining future pleasures is called '*Vorfreude.*' The opposite is called anxiety. What sounds more worth fantasizing about? Whether an experience bites you or blesses you makes absolutely no difference. But how you envision it pre-destines your entire emotional experience until that moment.

I'd safely guess it's evident that you're more likely to fail if you practice envisioning the worst-case scenario. Alternatively, meditating on the best case scenario moves you with greater confidence towards that end. All we know is that you're better off when you don't assume the worst. Just because the worst-case scenario is emotionally provocative doesn't mean it is the most likely.

My anger and passion in this chapter are in how casually we forgot to consider the life-altering experience our neighbour could bestow on us if we were only receptive enough. If you lose your romanticizing of curiosity in the smallest things, then all small significances will pass you by.

It's no wonder why we are bored. We are disconnected from our sense of awe.

Perhaps we fear that we are the boring ones. That still means we are in charge of creating ourselves to be somebody of interest that people wish they could bump into along their strange journeys. We all create job resumes, but few of us create life resumes. How do we pitch the goodness of our own life to ourselves? If we can't exude our enthusiasm and passions as a homing beacon for other awesome people, no kidding, we feel lonely.

In the next chapter, I will expand on the universal power of balance and the absurd paradox of how we grow. It brings the roadmap of action to those three fundamental perspectives of what is, what we think it ought to be, and how we can make it so. If we can understand this one law that governs so much of our experience, we can teach ourselves to chase our desires with precision and clarity. Then, we can teach it to everybody else who feels lost along the way. The whole game changes when you discover how much control you have in transforming yourself.

Ain't no more time for acting like we don't know what we can do! If we dare take the first step, the world is prepared to conspire in our favour.

CHAPTER 11

Let's Talk Freedom

I imagine self-esteem issues were not plaguing the man, Genghis Khan. Or, perhaps this was, in fact, the driving force behind his barbaric conquests? However, I can but only speculate what motivated the heart of such a bloodthirsty conqueror.

If you aren't yet familiar with Genghis Khan, he's second to top on the list of most relentless conquerors in the world. A recent post suggested if he were to be ranked for net worth by modern metrics, his dynasty of controlled territory would place him at approximately 100 trillion dollars.

The most relevant words spoken alongside the name of Genghis Khan are typically 'brutal,' 'pillage,' and 'rape.'. Eventually, you will also hear him called 'intelligent' and 'tactically masterful.' This guy was essentially one of the ultimate human monsters by most measurements. But he was still human. That means many more 'Genghis Khan' like-minded individuals could roam the earth now. Thankfully, our world's military capacity can stop such evil much faster than the days of war by sails and horseback. Apparently 7% of the world's population has lineage through Genghis Khan. That doesn't mean all his descendants are so cruel. In fact, Genghis Khan's mindset may have exclusively died with him. Better yet, others have risen to defy people like this before they ever had a chance.

I started with the probability he didn't have self-esteem issues because he was nothing special by creation. He was human, like me and you. I think a big difference is somewhere along the line that Genghis stopped asking, 'Can I?' and started asking, 'How can I?' Genghis was well in tune with his freedom and took full advantage of it. He was free to be a monster. Others were free to try and stop him. He equipped himself with brilliant wit, unwavering dedication, and unfaltering faith in his vision. I'd safely give those same qualities to anybody who's left a mark in history.

Genghis Khan, Martin Luther King Jr., Hitler, Nelson Mandela, Marcus Aurelius, Abraham Lincoln, Gandhi, and many more. Not names you typically see in the same list, but they were all very aware of their freedom. Some arguably more or less so than the next. Some are the oppressors; others are the oppressed. But all: Free. Whether conquering countries, reforging human rights, slaughtering millions, or being confined to stone walls for decades, they maximized their freedom. Never a 'Can I?' Only 'How Can I?' No matter their circumstances.

They were all the heroes of their own story and were convinced their work was righteous. Some we agree, others we do not. There are only combating forces of ideology, and both the evil and the righteous are vanquished - no matter which way you look at it. The only pathetic thing is to do nothing. In a world where freedom wages war against other's freedom, doing nothing is the recipe for victimhood.

Of course, not all are made for war. But freedom raises many conversations, and every single one of them is a call to action.

Paradox of Everything

Your ability to create a reality is proportional to your willingness to experience its opposite. The cliche, 'Break yourself to build yourself up,' is the soul of this process. The irony of desire is that it captivates a sense of lack. Feeling lacking because of a longing for something suppresses the goodness of what you already have. Where is your line of true contentment? At what point do you consider more happiness bonus material?

I'll rapid-fire some examples to illustrate how this paradox is a common thread throughout life.

You don't have energy because you've practiced laziness and inaction. You gain more energy by using up what you already have in your reserves. You amplify endurance by reaching the end of your durability. You grow your muscles by stressing them and making micro-tears that create space for strength to be woven into your muscle fibres. Your reluctance to be seen as weak in the gym keeps you from becoming strong.

You get broke by acting rich when that isn't your reality. You get rich by living like you're broke while you save money.

Managing too many casual, shallow friendships doesn't make space for deep connections. Boundaries that keep many out will make you feel alone while you create space for deep, powerful relationships.

Acting like you don't have trauma or flaws makes them more obvious to others. Trying to hide insecurity steals time from you acting on your talents and gifts. Digging up your trauma will make you feel broken while you begin healing.

Acting like you have all the answers can cripple your intelligence and potential to learn. Your willingness to expose your gaps of understanding allows you to be receptive to new wisdom.

Thinking your way is the only way will soon have you outsmarted and outdated. Your humility to gain other perspectives allows your creativity to pioneer new ideas and keep up with the times.

You will feel powerless and without peace in proportion to how much control you expect to have over your life. You discover how powerful and at peace you are when you are not emotionally attached to managing others and outcomes. *That which knows how to bend will not break.*

Desiring love insinuates you are without love. To love yourself and be content in your own space makes you more desirable to be around. Others can sense your stability. So, if you are stable before they arrive, they can amplify what you have already created, lest you lose your power and leave your well-being in another person's hands. Nobody has any obligation to love or support you. That's the only way love and admiration are worth something.

Your envy and jealousy devalue everything you have. Gratitude makes the most out of little. The easiest thing in the world is to stop being grateful for something you think isn't going to disappear. Although something may not last, acting in gratitude sustains its value.

Your ego and desire for special treatment will make your presence a burden. Your humility to be equal amplifies how special and complimentary your true value is.

Your gluttony and greed insinuate your lack even when you have too much. Service and selflessness will convince your body, mind, and soul that you have enough to give and share even when you have little.

Feeding an unhinged anger is the fastest way to increase the lack of justice in the world. Your patience despite wrath is how you calculate and maximize the potential of that chaotic sensation.

Only considering the final result as a win insults the entire journey. You must grow comfortable making countless mistakes in learning a new language, honing a new talent, and creating new science and technology. Everything wonderful and worthy is on the other side of diligent effort in loving the process over the results. If you can enjoy the process of fumbling forward, all victories along the way are sweet celebrations despite a final goal that can't be promised.

Perhaps the most significant paradox is being unwilling to sacrifice lesser-quality habits to make time for better ones. This is the most accurate measure of your willpower and faith. Sacrificing lesser healthy things for the better should be our most sensible act. It is our personal gamble with the universe. This exact choice is how we disrupt the universe's flow and become the interruption that shifts the unfolding of things. This practice captivates the most scary and exhilarating essence of the human experience.

Every single one of these examples is within your capability. It's doable today. Like fear is our sharpest definition, we are made new with every mental and emotional wall we break through. Now, with this foundation laid, I get to be a bit more sassy.

I Swear If You Say 'Can't' One More Time…

Let's talk about how free you are—I mean *really* free. Freedom is the default operation of our lives. The only thing to negotiate is *how* freely you're willing to act out your own life. All we do is negotiate with the consequences of our freedom. Let me draw it out.

You are free to get a financial loan. You are free not to pay that loan and face the consequences. You are free to stop eating breakfast every day. You are free to never talk to your friends again. Same with your enemies. You're free to commit your life to somebody. You're free to betray that person. You are free to tread through private property. You are free to design a rocket. You are free to have countless children or none. You are free to write a book or a song. You are free to live entirely off the land and be a ghost of society. You are free to be the influencer who shifts the entire system. You bargain with the consequences of that choice. Whether you succeed is on the far end of the conversation. The main issue is a world full of people terrified to try.

Whenever I talk to anybody trying to make a beneficial change in their lifestyle, if I hear, "I can't…" I interrupt the conversation. You *can*. I don't care what it is. The thing is, people don't have intentional conversations about what's *not* possible. 'Can't' is a statement of powerlessness. That has nothing to do with you. What *can* you do?

Every monumental change in human history defied what we originally knew was possible. It was people who had conversations about *how,* regardless of the audacity that came with the rest of the world, assuming they were wasting time. All until the seas were sailed. Until the Skies were flown. Until the earth was mined. Until our organs were transplanted. Until we asked that special somebody on a date.

Ships sank. Airplanes crashed. Men were buried under the earth. Some didn't survive their essential surgery. Some of us got rejected. Failure is the only thing that makes freedom free. Without fear, there is no courage. Without suffering, there is no thriving. Without loss, there can be no gratitude. Without shortcomings, there is no humility. Without forces fighting against us, there is nothing worth fighting for. It is only because we have no idea why we are here that we are allowed to live on purpose. Only in the void of meaninglessness can we decide our own worthiness and bring value to intention. Every action in this life is a rebellion against the powers that wish to diminish us.

I am free to write whatever I want here. So to you, I say, *skoobidee-bap, baby*. I bargain with the consequences of *every single sentence*. I risk offending somebody or mishandle a topic not represented from every angle. I am free to mess this up and not invest every fibre of my effort and pawn it off as human error if I do something poorly. Or I can write a lifeline and rally a higher quality of well-being if I can only live it out myself first and share my journey transparently.

You're free to take what you need and discard the rest. You're also free to bitch and moan as if I offended you personally despite my saying over and over that I want every individual to be truly free, harmonious, powerful and authentic. You can rest easy that I will also face the positive and negative consequences of everything I stand for.

There is a psychological experience called 'choice paralysis.' It's the idea that we have so many options that we overthink to the extent of doing nothing. All because of fear that choosing wrong outweighs the possibility that we choose the right thing. In addition, when we quickly decide and are left staring at all the options we missed out on, we may be less satisfied because we focus on the lack. We entirely forget we were lucky enough to have an option in the first place.

Pride and ego love options and wallow in roads left untraveled. Gratitude understands you cannot walk two paths at once. Even having options in the first place is a form of fortune. *Perspective, amigo!*

If you come to a genuine conclusion that you *cannot* do something, that is also a victory of clarity that something has run its course. You either make peace with changing your goals, or you wage war against the odds with what unlikely steps are still possible. Inaction is also a choice. You'll have to make peace with the consequences of that, too.

Surrendering and powerlessness can be confused as the same thing. But those who know how and what to surrender understand the power of their time and energy. There is strength in surrendering a battle that no longer serves you. An example of a stupid game that wins stupid prizes is being caught up in revenge. Surrendering can become the strongest move to be bigger than a petty war. We are as big as the problems we give our time to. Giving all our attention to pathetic problems makes us feel pathetic because we realize how small the battle that we are fighting is.

'Can't' is a story-killer. It smothers hope. It's a buzzkill. It's an admittance of fear. It's a revealer of priorities and how much you actually care. It is the lube for your weak excuses to separate you from things you actually want but are afraid to fight for. The walls of your comfort zone are intricately decorated with the excuses you've created to validate them.

My friend said she 'can't stop apologizing' for what isn't her problem. So, whenever she says sorry when something isn't hers to apologize for, I have a trigger word: "Turtles." It recalls an inside joke between us about an interesting lady who tried to argue with religious leaders that the world is flat and on the back of a giant turtle floating through space. When they asked her what that turtle was standing on, she responded with zero hesitation.

"More turtles. Turtles *all* the way down."

So, we always laugh, and my friend is grateful that our trigger word genuinely helped interrupt her habitual apologizing. I'd suggest you grab a friend and find the best trigger word you can muster for when our shitty attitudes get in the way and we try pulling that lame 'can't' card. Let your trigger be a joyous reminder that you are free.

When you're forced to be honest with how often our 'can't' is more of an 'I don't want to' the whole game changes. If the 'I don't want to' translation doesn't make sense, it's because it reveals that you *want* the thing. Surrender or step up to the occasion.

We Love an Underdog

Why do we love stories of underdogs? Because we see ourselves in them. It doesn't matter if it's David vs. Goliath, the first black man to play pro baseball, 300 Spartans fending off a million Persians, or just a kind person with big dreams who's down on his luck. Heck, even the anti-heroes who are primarily portrayed as assholes and reluctant to do good are especially attractive stories to us. Why? Because it teeters on the idea of turning your back on a broken world after being wronged and proving we have redemption and selflessness in our bones. Despite everything that would justify us leaving the world to burn, we know something about it is worth preserving. Even if we don't know what that is yet.

We are as bold as any reason we define as compelling for ourselves.

We have a strange fascination with stories of greatly unlikely odds, yet somebody attempting to defy them. We either grin as if 'they still got this,' or our heart sinks because of the possibility of true misfortune that sometimes the bad guy win. But we are invested and do not wish that to be true. Why? We are reflecting our own story in emotions. And what is the secret sauce before the climactic battle?

The ultimate doubt.

Utter devastation. Losing every reason to fight. Being as weak as we've ever been before facing down insurmountable odds. What is the 'turning point' for our hero? A decision that enough is enough. Sheer willpower and a full captivation of the present moment.

If nobody else, why not us? Even if it kills us, we fought for something noble and on purpose. We justify every moment we've endured to bring ourselves to such moments.

Ok, that's fantastic and all, but when will our great adventure be bestowed upon us? That's where the movies have us fooled. It suggests people are bestowed their journey. So, we wait for ours. We end up glorifying shallow drama in the absence of a real adventure because it's the wildest thing we currently have going.

Otherwise, we rave about the worldly news. Got nothing interesting in your own life? Complain. What else? It makes you sound passionate like you give a damn! Like you're an activist! Until the conversation of freedom calls us to action, and we pawn it off to people who 'are more capable' or 'directly affected.' Because the problem is just too big for little ole you, right? We justify it. We strengthen our fear to act by remaining an observer of this great big world.

The audacity we have to make a difference in the grand picture is the journey we can bestow on *ourselves*. Pick a problem and do *something*. *ANYTHING!* Anything that bugs you *is* what beckons you!

But we are holding out for 'our' journey, aren't we? Because we can stay comfortable yet and hold out until something bigger and 'story worthy' comes our way. Which rarely or never does. So, we meet the end of our livelihood chalk full of regrets, exaggerated stories and bitterness. Are we even *less* than an underdog to not even deserve a story-worthy life?

Not so.

The super secret sauce hidden in the movies is there for us to learn from but always escapes us. It is that the underdog either decided or genuinely did not have a choice.

Even if they *had* a choice, the consequence would be something quite dire beyond redemption to walk away from. Otherwise, they would be forfeiting their story-worthy life. That alone is drive enough to take a risk. That element easily escapes us in this squishy, modern world of instant pleasures. Many of my friends who 'stumbled' upon being impact players in this world dug themselves out of rock bottoms through addictions and destructive behaviours that spiralled their world out of control. They were met with a pre-climactic moment. It is a bold decision when there is nothing else to lose, and despite every reason to give up, there is something worth fighting for. And that's enough.

That sounds glamorous until the raw details sound like failed suicide attempts. Laying in the hospital bed after taking too many pills and having to teach yourself how to speak again. It looks like eating disorders, drunken rages, broken hearts, and minds consumed by depression and anxiety. Sometimes, existence feels like bouncing between different forms of suffering and trying to spend time in which suffering hurts the least.

These stories aren't so movie worthy when the gritty details boil down to internal warfare of lacking purpose, meaningful connection, and reason to live. We lose ourselves in whatever convinces our minds to be pleasurable. We eventually meet our pre-climactic moment: Sheer willpower and full presence to entirely suck the marrow out of life. To fully own our freedom. We deny ourselves all our self-serving and destructive habits to find ourselves lost and scared in new, unexplored experiences. And it's enough.

Speaking from personal experience, shared quite thoroughly in *An Arsenal of Gratitude*, it is excruciating to have your story-worthy life be a battle against yourself. It's riddled with shame, guilt, bitterness, resentment, envy, jealousy, and so on. Every emotion in our experience is meant to teach us something. All those awful feelings are actually our body trying to heal itself.

It's a constant question: 'Why do we feel this pain? How do we stop it?' The answers tend to always revolve around gratitude, humility, practicing presence, compassion, love, and courage. Most other positive emotions stem from those elements.

It seems like a very small story and battle to wage war against. But our story is the story of the human experience. If we suffer from our own conditioning, so do others. When we transform our suffering into lessons that that limit the suffering of others, we suddenly go from being small-minded to living large as life.

Ego is the story of 'me.' Humility is the story of 'we.'

Rising to the occasion is a strange phrase of speech. Our spirit already received all the permission we needed at birth. Our life *is* the occasion. When we get out of our own way, the whole world happens *for* you, not to you.

I'm pissed off that we missed a very strange and beautiful revelation of how much power we have here. The entire universe is unfolding exactly as intended with its natural order. All except for one species. Us. We are the disturbance in otherwise perfectly fine order that will go on with or without us. We are intelligent enough to bargain with the future and align ourselves to follow out tasks no other species can compare. Our ego created its own perspective of self-importance that convinced us that the world is against us. If we are that smart, we can chip away with logic until we understand it is all *for* us.

As I contemplated the possibility that I could very well meet any fatal end while horseback guiding off-grid, merely being off-grid made me 'dead' to the modern world. If I died, in other's minds, I could still be alive until they discovered otherwise. Everything is an assumption until it becomes a fact.

For anything that is not factual, like our perspective of the universe and our role in it, we can decide whatever we want our relationship with it to be. If it doesn't take you seriously, that is permission enough to have fun with it. It is all a play. Your role is whatever you choose.

Change yourself, hire your friends, and fire those who do not serve your greatest good. Take the biggest breath you've ever taken and make a decision you've never made before. Spite the odds—or don't. I'm just sick of people thinking they aren't free.

Get weird with it. If you wanted a sign, this is it.

CHAPTER 12

Big Gift Energy

I allow myself at least one deep, unapologetic liberty per creation. So please allow, or perhaps forgive, the crude humour that is about to ensue. I intend to dance a fine line of provocative and wholesome content here. Some readers might find the analogies off-putting, but like comedy, that's the edge you play to be memorable, entertaining and educational all at once. You also wouldn't respect it if I played it safe on a book about fear, would you?

There is a cultural term that has sprung up over the past few years called 'Big Dick Energy.' It suggests somebody is in tune and unapologetic with their presence and value as if born lucky. But it is evident that people with big dicks can be cowards, and people with smaller dicks can be courageous. So, what exactly is Big Dick Energy? (I'll switch this to big 'gift' energy, which is universal for my metaphors. But I have no intention to tone down the phallic jokes.)

This term is not gender specific as everybody is equally capable of having a magnetic and grounded sense of their potential. Additionally, Big Vagina Energy doesn't exude the same expression. Big Gift Energy is the insinuation that you are appropriately and harmoniously using your God-given gifts and talents. But even more importantly, you can compose this sort of energy *despite* your deficiencies or shortcomings.

Big Gift Energy has nothing to do with any actual physical features. It is more a spirit of how one composes oneself. It is a balanced confidence, self-assuredness, and calmness in one's own capabilities. It is intrinsic charisma that does not need to brag or boast, nor does it fear allowing others to have the spotlight. Just like having an actual big gift doesn't need to go around belittle any smaller gift in comparison.

The symbolic potential is nearly endless here. Buckle up because I can bridge the understanding of privilege, relationships, and spirituality all with Big Gift Energy.

Big Gift Privilege

Big Gift Energy is the bane of acting privileged. However, just like privilege, you're the worst if you flaunt it in hopes of making others feel inferior. It is the fact that you have been granted something of value that gives you the potential and/or position to make the human experience better for others. Knowing how to actualize and use your gifts accordingly provides that magnetizing and grateful radiance. May our blessings never exceed our virtues.

Our gifts, talents, and potential are all unique and not always obvious. Still, if you expect praise and an easier life for something you didn't earn - which is the definition of privilege - you're an especially disappointing person. It is in humility that your gifts are accentuated because it is not desperate for approval. This amplifies your sense of self-worth, knowing you have the autonomy and value to know and choose what is good for you.

When you are maximizing yourself as a person, others of optimal intent will gravitate to you. Rather than scrape at any opportunity that comes your way, Big Gift Energy is a state of integral abundance.

People of privilege often don't always recognize their position since it is their state of normalcy. They don't have a window into what it is like until their benefits are taken from them. Much like somebody with a big gift may not understand any anxiousness in their performance until they experience a dysfunction. When they cannot lean on their privilege, do they crumble and feel sorry for themselves? Or do they realize they are made up of many more things that compose their quality of character? That is the integral abundance of Big Gift Energy.

If you feel sorry for yourself when losing your privilege, then by default, you must feel pity for those without ever having the privilege, no? In this, humility of your gifts is essential, knowing you are as vulnerable as everybody else. You can be deeply in tune with your vulnerabilities and not have them weaponized against you. If people come insulting and slandering your name as if to diminish your gifts, *why* would you ever truly be diminished if you know what you have to offer is incredible? Anybody who takes the time to know you and respects how you compose your own experience is who is meant for you. Anybody who buys into the slander is simply missing out on your gifts.

You are under no obligation to use your gifts to defy doubters. Your lack of defensiveness clarifies your confidence. Anyone who chooses to take one quality about you and alter it against you is expressing such insecurity that they hope to level the playing field by diminishing your light. Their offence to your gifts is just a confession of how small they feel in comparison.

On that note, I am anti-comparison but pro-competition. Somebody who is actualizing their gifts in a humble and integral manner understands the finiteness of their power. Big Gift Energy does not boast or hoard more than it can handle. Just like no individual has the potency and energy to sustain countless partners. It is more admirable to optimize meaningful relationships. Hell, people doing their best have enough difficulty with one partner. Big Gift Energy is not intimidated by competition but rather conspires with the best of others to optimize potential and enthusiasm across the collective.

It would seem appropriate to be frustrated with somebody who had obvious gifts and refused to use them. It can be a loving sentiment to want somebody to recognize everything they have in their favour. Yet, we are not responsible for others' commitment to their insecurity. Big Gift Energy is something that each one of us has to earn individually.

Big Gift Energy is actualized self-love in motion. In that, Big Gift Energy transcends privilege. In fact, it may be your lack of privilege that accentuates the magnitude of your energy. You are a living example of defying the odds. How you spite all the reasons you have to justify your insecurity builds the foundation of your magnificence.

Big Gift Relationships

In a literal and figurative sense, men with smaller gifts may fear it will affect their performance and, therefore, their partner's satisfaction. If you do not have much to offer in a competitive dating market, no kidding, you would fear those who clearly have more to offer. If you are not maximizing your life experience, I believe that is *exactly* what should merit your insecurity.

Gift size aside, if you're boring, no kidding, you'd be threatened by anybody who finds ways to milk the joy of everything life offers. You don't need a massive gift to penetrate life's experience deeply. All you need is a sense of curiosity, direction, and bravery to be more interesting than most people on earth. Simply being enthusiastic about your own life and having the ability to share that on a mental, emotional, sensual and spiritual level is the gift you have to share. If you allow an insecurity of one individual element of your reality to diminish your zest for life as a whole, you've done your entire life a disservice.

As a byproduct of Big Gift Energy, you will have a more refined sense of who can truly appreciate what you have to offer. When you are aligned with what stokes and sustains the fire of your lifestyle, you don't humour and try to force incompatible people into it. In fact, acting as if you are somebody whose time and energy are worth earning makes those who work for it more grateful for you.

If you act like a desperate, endless supply of admiration and energy, you can't expect anybody to respect what they didn't ask for. Just because you're offering somebody something doesn't mean they've confirmed they value what you're giving. That is a quick path to resenting people, though it would be misplaced, considering you didn't even ask them if they value what you're pushing on them.

Big Gift Energy doesn't feel the need to justify itself. It's an individualized prowess that sets you outside the cultural bubble and sends you into a league entirely of your own. Nurturing your own gifts creates a beacon where people who can compliment and be complimented by your existence can find you. If you lack an identity, values and direction, then you are absolutely in the cesspool of societal mediocrity. Big Gift Energy is the essence of your authentic expression. Being that person gives everybody around you permission to actualize their authenticity.

So, how do we go about that?

Big Gift Spirituality

How does one justify their own existence? Well, you get to face and ponder some serious questions and challenges. What did you expect? If you want to behold an aura of magnitude, you can't be a poser. You have to be weathered and scarred by having lived out genuine adventure in which to uphold your character and confidence. You can't fake Big Gift Energy. Even if you can for a time, it might be justice that you will inevitably watch the best things in your life disown you for being a coward in conqueror's clothing.

By definition, the meaning of life is whatever *meaning* you give *your* life. If you can enthusiastically live out whatever meaning you've established, you are free to wrap your essence around it. Just be prepared to have to mature and outgrow inferior lifestyles for something new and of greater purpose.

Being reluctant to upgrade your purpose as it presents itself is like getting mad at yourself for being aroused by an opportunity. It is a literal and figurative failure of 'rising to the occasion.' Because you're too afraid to perform in a more meaningful manner than self-fondling.

If you can't surrender to the vulnerability of life's great opportunities, you can't expect to feel life's ultimate pleasures. The risks are significant, but so are the rewards.

Big Gift Spirituality is trusting that you are divinely guided. It is faith that your best intent will constantly be stress-tested and corrected so you can fumble forward in a worthwhile fashion. It is to act in such a courageous manner that your own suffering and direction justify themselves.

Big Gift Spirituality is having a core way of acting in the world as if your movement is in alignment with something as powerful as that which made all of existence. It's incredibly difficult to shake the spirit of somebody who believes they are favoured by existence itself. You would act as if all turmoil and tragedy are inadvertently conspiring to call the best out of you.

As you turn life into a playground of self-discovery for your gifts, you will inevitably face how they affect others. Bravery is whatever stretches your personal capacity. But on a communal scale, bravery can only be proportional to the normalcy around you. So, there can be a culture of cowardice with a low bar for somebody to be impressive. Do you want to be a big fish in a small fishbowl? Or a big fish in the great big ocean? It may be up to you to defy your communal expectations and venture into a new world where your calling is more appropriate and appreciated.

Big Gift Self-Acceptance is knowing that your life's calling also factors in your defects and inefficiencies. Your ability to be in tune with your vulnerabilities and ignorance allows you to have empathy and connection with all the other imperfect yet perfectly capable people.

There may be qualities, insufficiencies, and a track record of experience that may feel justified to disqualify you from what you deem an incredible life. How could somebody as impure as you and I ever truly believe that goodness and fortune are not only real but actively seeking us? The truth is that the goodness and fortune of the world is ever-present. But we can outrightly reject it out of self-pity, guilt, shame, and fear that we will mishandle goodness as we have before.

To be fundamentally ordinary but act in extraordinary ways is how you as a person expose others' relationships with *their* potential, too. Others who aspire to activate their potential will gravitate to you. Others who allow their bitterness to be their guiding compass only confess their own lack of self-acceptance.

Just because others are confessing their spiritual gifts feel small does not mean you have to shrink yours to make them feel less pathetic. They already felt that way. They reflect their self-worth as if to place themselves under your shadow. However, your light, like breaking through clouds after a week-long storm, exposes them. You have your own obligation to shine and not apologize, just like the sun does not apologize for hurting our eyes. Cracking people's bitter composure is exactly where our light breaks in.

Love is a war waged exclusively by the wounded. Those fundamental vulnerabilities and weaknesses that make us feel unworthy are exactly how love is a lifestyle of bravery. To love and accept yourself is to understand that even with every reason you have to act small, there is enough substance worth being bold. In fact, the stories of the underdog are the anthem of humanity's bravery.

The same rule that makes good writing is what makes a heroic life story. The size of the problem or goal, compared to how small and pathetic the main character is, is how epic the adventure is. The courage to rise to the occasion and *become* who is needed to surpass the climactic challenge is the substance of a worthy story. It couldn't possibly matter how powerful or pathetic you are if you have no goal and substantial place to channel your gifts. This is what it is to be a grower, not a shower.

#GrowerNotAShower

We all start off vulnerable and useless. Some of us eventually grow to a status, physique, or presence that seems innately impressive or attractive in our given culture. That does not mean those people are pleased or content with their lives. Their outward appearance may be ideal to others, yet their internal satisfaction with their existence could be utter turmoil. If somebody's state of life produces lukewarm or half-mast enthusiasm, the signs are evident that they aren't fully actualized.

When was the last time you had your own joy, excitement, love, or laughter overwhelm you? Joy can be overwhelming, too! Enthusiasm is meant to be genuinely consuming. It seems only fair that if problems can be overwhelming, then the goodness of the world and what inspires you can do the same. How we captivate and translate that sensation is where our calling beckons us. Essentially, just like an ideal erection, your spirit is enthralled against its will towards that which genuinely excites you.

The moments and tasks that fully captivate our being into the present moment is where our potential can be activated.

You might argue, *'But Remmy, I'm fully 'in the moment' when I'm wasted, watching a good movie, watching porn, or playing a video game.'*

Okay, Sure. Are you harvesting benefits from your focus, or is somebody benefiting from harvesting your focus? You can do whatever you want, but all I ask is that you are capable of bragging to your loved ones about the honest details of your day. Is your enthusiasm self-serving, or is it evolving the well-being of those around you?

Imagine you decide instead of paying for any of the above services with money, you pay for them with your soul, your time, and your will to live. What's the difference? It took your soul, your time, and your will to live to make your money. It's only because you underestimate your soul, your time, and your life's value that you could spend it cheaply.

If you took a step back and thought for just one moment:

Holy sweet creation, I could be anybody and anything if I had the balls to work for it. If I had the humility to suck at something new and suffer the growing pains of something I deem worthwhile, it's mine to fight for. I am not promised a victory, but I can promise myself a life of curiosity and adventure if I wasn't so fucking afraid.

I would rather be terrified of not knowing what I am capable of. I want to fail and be rejected by things I find exciting and worthwhile instead of being cock-blocked by my own insecurity. I want to arrive in the world and let it say 'no' to me instead of me saying no to myself. I refuse to exist in mediocrity and normalize anything that only gives me half a boner's worth of excitement about my own existence. My joy and my enthusiasm are my own damn responsibility. I am free. I am free. I am free.

I may not entirely believe myself to be of massive value or importance, but I want to know what happens when I start showing up and acting like I am. I did not ask for this body, this mind, or this soul. Time is ticking, and I want this briefness to be a dare for how much sweetness and magic I can sow into existence.

I want to chew slowly and taste my fucking food instead of being haunted by all the things I haven't yet achieved and may not get to experience. Where I am today must be enough because it is what I must work with. I want to breathe deeply, take it all in, and remember where I came from when I'm baffled by how far I can go, only mere days, weeks and months from now.

I want to arrive on my final day and make Death himself flinch. May I act with the appropriate amount of pride for the depth and vastness of my experience. May my crow's feet be deep and obvious for all the joy and laughter I found. May I never lose touch with the weird, impossibly unique gift that is this life and those I saw it through with. May I have a humble relationship with my vulnerabilities and high-five God at the pearly gates. Let the gates blast open so even somebody like me with my timid voice can join the choir of angels who sing that there is bravery in this world.

May this collection of imperfections that is my life be a showcase of fumbling forward with grace and grit. May I wrestle with God as a sign of respect and receive discipline with class when I am to be corrected. May I not cling to what isn't for me and claw up worthy mountains step by step. May I never lose touch with how little I need to prosper and delegate my abundance in ways that can amplify the opportunity of others.

May it never be said that I was born magnificent. But rather that I was a grower, not a shower.

Chapter 13

Out of My League?

On which grounds do we decide we are lesser than and greater than somebody? You either have a million answers, or you're baffled by the question. In mere instances, we paint a vivid assumption of other's superiority or inferiority.

I grew up on this funny clichés like, *'If you're going to be dumb, you best be strong.'* So sometimes it's easy to fit dumb beside strength because what else could they offer? But if they end up witty and smart as well, we are a tad shocked, aren't we? being exceptional at one thing like physique is hard enough, so they probably sacrificed their education to look like that, right? Our doubts are riddled in every crack of our assumptions.

It makes sense to recognize a bloodthirsty soldier from a warring nation as fast as possible so we can flee. But looking across the room at a beautiful person and deciding that you are immediately unworthy is frankly bullshit. This emotion from a second of calculation tells a story far bigger than that instant of self-imposed unworthiness.

The only information in that specific scenario of seeing a beautiful person is that you find them attractive. That's it. All other assumptions and computations will play with your sense of adequacy or lack thereof. You *can't* assume that his or her tattoos make them unrelatable. Or that they don't share the same values, spirituality, or whatever other nonsense you made up in that instance. Everything you conjure up as reasons *not* to approach that person is purely out of self-inadequacy. Your closed-off thinking never allowed you to go and be surprised by somebody's true nature.

I reiterate that I am anti-comparison but pro-competition. Competition is the reason we strive at all. Being able to discriminate is one of our most valuable functions because we have to be able to maintain a standard of ourselves. If we can't say no to what we don't want, we have no power or value in our decisions. You're a human doormat if you are afraid to say no and hold to your standard. We do not have unlimited amounts of anything to give, so offering the right thing to the right people and making the most harmonious relationships is the goal. But being too insecure to initiate anything is the real problem at hand here.

We may always be prey to our limited understanding, but we can checkmate our thoughts. We can shift our intentions to summon courage to smite our bullshit thinking. But first, let's actually face the immediate calculations of inadequacy we can sense through visuals alone.

How To Lose Before You Start

If that person you find attractive has impressive physical features, it may reflect that you know you could be in better shape yourself. If their presentation seems to state a value of theirs, then they may reasonably expect the same from an ideal partner. We are a living sales pitch of ourselves at almost all times. Whether we like it or not. That emotional reaction is saying you see the price they paid, and you're unwilling or have not yet paid the price to meet their portrayed value. It is in your power to make yourself adequate under that light.

If that person wearing lavish brands and heavy jewelry intimidates you, it may reflect your lack of financial abundance. Financial richness may be an expectation of theirs for you to meet them at their 'level'. If you desire a simplistic life, then that is actually more of a detriment to your values and should supersede mere attraction. Richness is a relevant perspective. If the value of abundance is not aligned, you're setting yourself up for failure. A thing you could never know until you go talk to them.

If that person presents themselves as intellectually powerful, you have no choice but to go pique their mind to ensure that assumption. It may reflect that you wish you had more education. You can do something about that. Perhaps they are exhausted by that side of their life and need somebody to teach them how to unwind and expand their adventurous side. You could be that person if you dared have a conversation with them.

If that person presents themselves as exotic and boldly different, you may reflect a sense of ordinary lifestyle that may not interest them. You might feel you have nothing to offer them regarding glamorous adventures and mystery. But what if that presentation of theirs represents their sense of being misunderstood? Perhaps they desire somebody who makes them feel seen, known and understood. All that unique style may be an arsenal of conversation starters! Don't submit to the intimidation of their expression if that inspires your interest. Allow the magnetization to work its magic and find out for yourself.

Any curiosity you have about them is a conversation opener. What if that person is actually so attractive that they are always approached for shallow reasons? What if nobody is giving them attention out of their equal sense of inadequacy? Therefore, your boldness to approach them would be all the more meaningful. No angle of thinking doesn't loop back to the logic of starting the conversation to satisfy your curiosity. It could be a few seconds that gives the rest of your day peace of mind. Alternatively, you win the next couple of weeks of anxiety of worrying, 'What could have been?'

Pronoia and believing the universe conspires in your favour must be met with a simple action on your curiosities. Maybe it becomes the conversation for hours that changes both of your lives. What if behind that fear is one of the most memorable and beautiful interactions you're yet to experience? All other alternatives teach you how to stifle your own desire and deepen your inadequacy. You either mount disbelief and fear in your soul or nurture the beauty of opportunity hiding behind every 'hello.'

Extensions of Ourselves

The purest form of confidence may be one (or both) of two things:

1. A complete sense of security and contentment with your own naked body.
2. The capacity to humour all other's opinions and perspectives without being provoked or disturbed by differences from yourself. Hold no attachment to any outcome, fully trusting the other's capacity to own their free will - rejection and all.

Let's start with the complete sense of security and contentment with your own body. I was born with a defect that the bones in my toes didn't fully grow. My big toes are normal, but the rest are essentially nubs without the second knuckle bone. Small enough to the point some don't even have toenails.

On top of that, my Reynaud's syndrome of poor circulation makes my hands and feet go purple at even slightly below room temperature. With the harmless fun of older siblings constantly joking about them, I imagined all others were doing the same. I've dug my toes into the sand at beaches and was always hyper-vigilant to avoid my defect being recognized.

Even good friends who've never noticed them before would be so shocked as to stop, point and exclaim, "What the fuck are *those*?!"

So, what are my options here? Do I diminish my own joy and lose full focus on the life in front of me because of some discoloration and abnormality? Or do I take off my fucking socks and dig my little toes into the sand and worry as little as everybody else?

To be fair, I'd also be concerned if I saw somebody else's feet were purple. So, the attention is of fairly genuine concern. Between the birth defect and discoloration from leukemia, I grew up with an ever-present concern-worthy feature to hide. So, I can't honestly say that I have utter contentment and security about the totality of my body. But I aspire to live despite those feelings and play to my heart's content. I am still fortunate to have functioning feet.

I return as much as possible to the resounding tone of my friend's argument, "No, *you* don't get it. Anybody who loves you doesn't care about your insecurity. They wonder why you aren't focusing on your gifts."

I'd be more embarrassed to admit on my deathbed that I didn't walk barefoot or go to the beach often because my little nubs are easy prey for a laugh. I might as well learn to laugh with them and remind myself how lucky I still am in the grand scheme of health. All other aspects are in my control to build a physique worth being proud of and enjoy the full span of a strong and healthy body.

As for the confidence and security of mind, curiosity is your ultimate friend here. This kind of confidence is having a friendly debate with someone who strongly disagrees with you—without feeling the need to prove them wrong or get defensive. You listen, maybe even laugh at some differences, and walk away with your peace intact, knowing their perspective doesn't threaten yours. Whether they agree with you or not doesn't shake your self-assurance.

An example of this confidence in intimate rejection is expressing your feelings to someone and genuinely being okay with whatever response they give—whether it's mutual or not. If they're not interested, you don't take it personally or let it shake your self-worth. Instead of feeling embarrassed or hurt, you respect their choice, wish them well, and move forward, knowing that the right connection won't require convincing. The difference of mutual excitement for one another rather than settling and tolerating one another is an entire world of difference.

I'll also be the first to admit that we can be all-consumingly excited about people who aren't wholly right for us. If we are starving, anything is better than nothing. But we need the self-value to eat alone rather than eat with the wrong people. Allow me to stress the value of quality connection over merely tolerating each other. Let me now elaborate on our Fast-food-style relationships.

McDonald's People

Imagine you're starving. I offer you steak (or whatever beautiful, healthy food if you're vegetarian) or McDonald's now; you'd likely say, "Give me McDonald's NOW!" Anything to stop this dramatic pain of starving. Physical starvation is similar to emotional and relational hunger in this regard. It manifests differently, but in the state of starvation, we tend to satiate the pain by any means necessary. Limiting pain is nothing to be ashamed of when it feels like you're dying. If you're on the brink of starvation, people claw at bugs or dangerous plants out of desperation.

Sometimes, our love lives aren't much different.

Some people may have been on a McDonald's equivalent of emotional satisfaction and be none-the-wiser. You might outrightly disbelieve that healthier relationships are possible if you've only ever had project partners. Project partners are people who we see and believe the best of, but only primarily receive their justified selfish behaviour, destructive habits and even abuse.

Until you experience a healthier meal, your body cannot fathom what it is like to run on better nourishment. It may even be in utter shock at first. But once you feel it, you realize all along and come to grips that your McDonald's diet is not the superior way to live.

When your life is surrounded by and deeply entangled with fast-food quality people, you either have to try bringing them with you to experience a healthier, more effortful life, or you must leave them behind. If you're so emotionally invested in them that you would abandon the chance at a healthier love life, then you keep them. End of story. You cannot maintain both. If you're afraid to end your fast-food relationships, your body, mind, and spirit will never properly acclimate to its potential and healthier life.

Loyalty is a virtue. But it becomes a detriment when it is something of poor quality, begging you to stay and not expose that it could also be healthier. Yes, higher quality is more effortful and expensive, but that's the universal price for quality. If you want quick fixes, there is no shortage of people who would love to treat your company cheaply and selfishly. But you abandon your right to complain after you experience that there are people who are willing and happy to put more effort into nurturing the right thing. You can't expect people you've given so much at a low investment to treat you like a high-value being.

And just like the analogy of steak or healthy vegan meals, there is a spectrum of higher quality as well. Higher quality comes in many flavours. You will inevitably know what makes you feel the healthiest once you sustain the diet long enough. But cheating on the diet and bitching about the results is your own fault. Whether in nutrition or love, we get what we put in. There is sometimes little or zero wiggle room for compromise of quality, but health and wellness outcomes are worth it.

Dare I ask, as I made this analogy, who came to mind in your life of who the 'McDonalds'' people are? Who are the fast-food fixes of connection that you know are not truly good for you but satisfy a need or desire at the moment? Are you that person for others? What would it take for you to commit and make space for a healthier emotional diet?

Here's the hardest part: You can't expect anybody honouring their healthy diet to take you seriously if you are afraid to leave your fast-food relationships behind. It's out of self-respect of their own standards to avoid what is evidently bad for your health and spirit. Sometimes solitude and taking care of yourself is the detox you need from fast-food people to make space for steak people.

Soul Food

In a world of people who are trying to be eye candy, try to be soul food. Eye candy is when people are the characteristic equal to a sugar fix. They are appealing and flavourful, but you will likely experience an energetic crash and can't live off it. On the other hand, soul food is when somebody is the characteristic equal to a homecooked meal. Leaving you healthier and happier afterwards. When it's good enough, you won't even crave the sugar fix anymore.

To develop your own flavour in the world and become soul food, you must nurture your own self and enthusiasm for life to your limits. You are a living sales pitch for yourself. Nobody can sell you better than yourself, so you might as well be thrilled about what you're selling! If you're lukewarm about your own experience, how could you possibly hope for anybody else to be overly thrilled about you when you aren't yourself?

It's beautiful that love makes us feel special when we rarely give ourselves that feeling. Sometimes it is the first time we consider ourselves special when another can feel it. But at the core, how could you sustain that if you've practiced belittling yourself? Another's love will land even harder and nurture you more deeply when you stop interrupting it. Giving that nourishment of love to yourself will help it not feel like such a foreign experience when somebody else comes around to share it with you.

If you're convinced that you aren't special, then you absolutely are in a competitive league of average people. I don't care if that bugs you. It should. Be angry enough to get excited about your own damn life. Do what thrills you, and quit apologizing. So, when somebody amazing comes around, you have ways to welcome them into the thrill of who you are.

Love has a way of making magic of the mundane. If you can do that with your own life, love is all the easier to experience and share. Romanticize your own life as if your happiness depends on it. Because it friggin does!

If you nurture your unique essence, you will become that unique individual outside of 'leagues.' You cannot be competed with because your flavour of loving and living has enough intricate detail to harmonize with a very specific kind of person. It is only a matter of finding that certain somebody of a common or complementary chord. But if you want to live the kind of life where you're earning a partner through status, material, or lifestyle, somebody is always richer and sexier to outbid you. Because here is the golden rule of love: I do not want somebody who does not want me.

Is somebody on the fence about you or another romantic option? Make it easy for them and leave. Valuing yourself enough not to be an option is how you attract those who don't hesitate.

Do not belittle your own zest for life by leaving it to somebody who treats it cheaply. The right person will love you to amplify what and who you already are. End of story.

A lukewarm expression of 'love' is not love at all. Love is a radical expression of nurturing the best of others. Be that soul food, the human embodiment of a homecooked meal, and that love will come to reciprocate the effort you are willing to give. You must maintain the backbone to reserve it for those who can reciprocate your effort. Let me show you how that is embodied into action.

Attraction, Negotiation, Maintenance

These are the three levels of a relationship's evolution. But they are all different skillsets. They must complement each other, and I will prove how this unfolds.

Attraction manifests in every way that you have value to portray and share. Whether it be money, physical beauty, humour, grand ambitions, a unique style, a powerful mindset, great storytelling, etc. It is usually one element that really captures somebody's attention and builds from that moment. Obviously, the more value, the merrier.

If you exclusively have the skill set to attract and amuse others without being able to ask what you want, you will be stuck with brief relationships. If you can tell others what you want, you must also be open to receiving and delivering on their desires. If you are exclusive to satisfying your own desires, then you end up in the realm of being a pickup artist or seductress. You cannot complain that you don't have lasting relationships if your priority is always your own pleasure.

When you become interested in a reciprocal, long-term dynamic, you can enter the negotiation stage. If you refuse to have the humility to be corrected and adapt to others' needs despite the cost or 'inconvenience,' then you can have real relationships. Some, maybe most, relationships are mutual benefit programs. *You get this, I get that.* The ultimate dynamic is that both participants are convinced they have the better end of the deal.

Most people are idealists and decent salespeople as far as negotiation goes. It is when your walk meets your talk that true maintenance is accomplished. You will have to revert to negotiate to reestablish a worthwhile harmony for all the ways your human imperfection and inconsistency are exposed. If you made a terrible sales pitch and cannot deliver on who you've portrayed yourself to be, the re-negotiations will become more difficult.

This is why loving your life and daily disciplines in solitude make maintenance easy with others. If you can share the evolution of your envisioned lifestyle, it is only a matter of growing alongside each other. If you cannot maintain your own ambitions, how do you think you could possibly manage another's desires and well-being into your mix?

When the shock of poor maintenance manifests, you or your partner must revisit negotiation if they are still attracted to each other. If that attraction can persist in the value you each perceive of one another, you can renegotiate. But if the attraction dies from inconsistency and failure to deliver, that's just emotional math playing out that you are not compatible as you negotiated. The more honest you are with your capabilities and humility, the more realistically you can negotiate.

If you ever wonder, 'How did we get here?' after a catastrophic relationship event, this three-step evolution will explain that: poor negotiation, inconsistency, selfishness, lack of maintenance, and unrealistic expectations.

These 3 skills can also explain the alternative of arriving at a beautiful, thriving relationship. You found somebody attractive, knew how to complement each other's well-being and goals, and delivered on that for one another. Whether love, friendships, or work, now you know how to make the magic happen.

Life in Colour

We don't know everything about ourselves, and we have been inside our minds and bodies our entire lives! Yet, we have the audacity to assume we know somebody else in a brief introductory conversation. Relationships take weeks, months, and years to reveal sides of ourselves that our partners haven't yet seen of us. The same goes for them to you. Some people are perfectly compatible in a season of life. They can act as the safety and support to maximize ourselves in a time that has to eventually end. The possibilities and dynamics are endless. Because the world has never seen what *you* are entirely capable of. We are as much of a statistic as we are the exception to every story. Humans have a nature, but our nature is also free will to defy the odds. Razzle-dazzle, baby!

Innocence, ignorance, chaos and goodness are playing in each of us all simultaneously. We can be inspiring, mesmerizing, a cautionary tale, a comedian, an artist, a broken spirit and an influencer all at once. And sorry (Not sorry), some people are just boring as cow crap. That's OK! Because somebody else just as boring to our perception would so love to share the simplistic company of the other 'boring' person. That doesn't mean they are in a lower league; they have different values. They might look at each other like God hand-crafted them for one another. They have a whole life to concern themselves about, and so do you.

Your job is solely to love yourself and your experience here. You'll feel like garbage if somebody you thought of as less-than suddenly found a love-on-fire before you did. Now, you're questioning everything about your own 'league' and self-worth. Because you made up leagues in your head and therefore placed everybody else in one. As soon as you see somebody is a 'lower league' get the outcome you are searching for, you have to put yourself in a lesser league by default of them having won the dumb game you made up in your mind.

The other people didn't even know they had a role in your weird ego game, and now their joy is your despair. This is all because of your sense of how things are meant to unfold went differently than you expected. That's a faulty version of *what is, how it ought to be, and how we are making it so*. If we weren't so obsessed with making up scenarios that made us feel right about how the world works, we would have more peace in the coming and going of life, love, and opportunity. We could even - and maybe should try to - celebrate how it unfolds for everybody else.

To really send this home, thinking of people in the sense of leagues is as dumb and damaging as being a racist. It's the same shallow game with assuming others are less-than, greater-than, and, at the core, divided for absolutely no good reason.

I'm pissed off that we have culturally allowed people to be judgmental cowards and play small because of it. We feed into each other's weak assumptions to cushion each other's lack of action. I'm pissed off that people are so emotionally obsessed with the possible pain of rejection that they forget they didn't have anything to lose in the first place. It's a self-imposed belittling of ourselves to sense a shred of excitement and be our own buzzkill before anything happens. We stifle our own adventure at the first glance of our souls being excited about something.

How insane that beauty alone can leave us so petrified and defeated based on our ability to consider ourselves worthy of it. We tell entire stories to ourselves, and we can be fundamentally changed if we listen to the beckoning of our intuitive interests. But instead, we... cower? It is literally woven into our nature to pass hundreds and thousands of faces and be surprised as we are captivated by only a few. Do not let the beauty in our unique design be stomped out by self-imposed inadequacy. You were born worthy of opportunity. Whether you act on that is the only difference.

Chapter 14

That Road to Hell

If a fiery hell must inspire us, perhaps we are not good people but bad people on a leash. If goodness for the sake of itself is not inspiring enough, the consequences of selfishness will leave us as a cautionary tale.

Picture this: Once upon a time, my friend knew something good was about to go down with a fine-looking lady nearing the end of a house party. This friend had more than enough to drink, not enough to be a mess, but dumb enough to drive drunk to get him and his new honey home. This was also *my* house party, and it's always been abundantly clear that there is zero tolerance for drunk driving. A *standard* per-say. Even if it's only a few blocks.

As we called him out, this friend knew what he did was wrong. There were about ten of us in a close friend group, and there was a bit of a debate on the repercussions of this act, regardless of his getting home safely. Some friends said a slap on the wrist was a good enough lesson because 'he *felt* bad.' I heard their arguments, but I thought it was rightly applicable that this friend had to be the designated driver for the next month. He was great about it and agreed to the terms.

This way, everybody won. A measure of justice is still laid down because even the best of us tend to push the boundaries of consequences. Especially if we successfully get away with a taboo act the first time. Human nature tends to realize they can get away with an inch and wonder if they can steal away with a mile. Perhaps not all people, but it becomes applicable with how we get too comfortable in relationships, professional shortcuts, a little white lie doesn't hurt anybody,' etc.

We will forever have a battle with grace and standards. It's a slippery slope. It's a weird gray area where so many seminars, books, mentors, and life experiences can only help so much before you must stare a moment in the face and draw your own line. Grace and standards are interchangeable with gratitude and divine anger here. I love my friend and welcomed him back with open arms - so long as he was the designated driver for a month. The grace in this gives the benefit of the doubt of his goodness, so I am grateful he rose to that goodness. The standard is not to let your friend drive drunk, whereas divine anger is the intensity with which I establish that justice.

He's never done it since, and we respect each other more for it. I have no problem being a buzz-kill if it means everybody's conscious is clear, knowing our friends get home safe. It doesn't matter how sexy and fast your car is if you get a DUI or killed.

That is all of our problems if we say we truly love that friend.

Standards Elevate Mankind

That fine line of peace of mind or 'How could this happen?' is good intentions and standards. I used to think that if somebody could see my heart and how badly I want to say and do the right thing, they wouldn't be so harsh and short-tempered. I wished for the benefit of the doubt. But as I hammer home in my last book, *the only valid apology is a change of behaviour.*

I realized a good intention is just a placeholder for a standard. If my good intentions mattered and my company desired the same thing, they would be willing to help it come to fruition. What is present at all times is our standards. *That* is what we stand on. A good intention is a fluffy fantasy until it is lived out.

That famous saying, '*The road to hell is paved with good intentions,*' never made sense to me until now. I felt like good intentions were valid in a world that just lacked patient communication. But actually, when we raise the bar and help teach healthy boundaries and a sense of self-worth, the game entirely changes.

What I mean is that my other young friend's good intentions not to be a lousy drunk mean nothing when his girlfriend is crying on the phone with 911, and he needs to get his stomach pumped. We know his good intentions meant absolutely nothing by the way he cracked a beer the following afternoon when he got out of the hospital. In addition, our good intentions to help him are gutless if we don't have the spine to tell him what an absurd line he crossed and draw a boundary. We need a new lived-out standard. Otherwise, he has a safe space to continue his recklessness when we are too quick to forgive. It's no longer just about him; all of us are playing as silent participants in a deepening alcoholism.

That road to hell was laid by his lack of ownership and by our flimsy backbone that didn't hold him to it. We failed to say, 'That shit does not fly in our home.' All of our grace will strike us like lightning when the day comes that 911 doesn't come fast enough to pump his stomach the next time. If we don't live to a healthy standard and make our friend's sobriety as soft of a journey as we can today, then there is no promise that his demise will not force us to be far less graceful next time.

I also newly understood God as one word: Consequences. People who are truly trying to be their best selves and take courageous steps in the universe have a deep respect for consequences. It's only people who prefer their lies and victimhood that think the world is supposed to fall in their lap. Those people build a pathetic, cowardly relationship with consequences. 'Woe is me,' they say.

If you play stupid games and win stupid prizes, then that means the universe is well and in order. That is what is meant by being a God-fearing person. If the universe has an order, it means dumb deeds deserve dumb rewards. If we want to harmonize with the universe, we don't try or desire to be outside the fair consequences.

If you want to scare yourself straight, you might wish for pure results—minimal universal grace. Let's try this thought experiment.

I Wish You a Fair World

Imagine if you are slightly impaired and drive; you are promised a minor fender-bender. If you are moderately impaired and drive, you are promised a broken bone. If you are highly impaired and drive, you are promised to lose a loved one, end up handicapped or die.

Would you want this world? Or would you prefer a free-willed world where we bargain with every word, every step and every moment? We would have to bargain with our desires and moderate one another in a world of endless possibilities of great serendipities and tragedies. If it were all black and white, there would be no wonder, mystery, or luck to be surprised by.

Maybe some of you might like the security of a graceless world. However, we live in a free world where we have to align ourselves with our potential and truly roll the dice. Only this way can we be spontaneous and stumble upon miracles and the unexpected. I would personally argue that the world of the unknown will always reign superior.

It's when people cheat, lie, steal, and manipulate the odds unjustly that the world feels corrupt. But the forces of good, once again, must be meaner than evil. When evil tries to ask for an inch but steals away with the mile, our standards of self-respect and boundaries fend off that evil. The universe and karma pull a lot of weight, but we as people have a role among one another to toe the line and create our own justice. If people do not want to cooperate with that harmony, we must love our values enough to keep our distance or demand better. If they are a true friend, they will meet you at a higher standard. They would not mope and whine that you desire better for them and yourselves.

On top of that, many of us are too broke to afford therapy. We have to minimize needless trauma the best we can. Often, all we have is each other to console when somebody's ignorance creates meaningless tragedy.

Where Values and Standards Collide

A standard is exposed in two ways:

1. When you are uncomfortable enough to make a difference. (The low end)
2. The most pleasant quality of character and happiness you are *willing* to maintain. (The high end)

There is a space between the high and low end of our standards where our life exists. Inside of that space is our reality. Everything outside of that reality is either a problem or a fantasy. I would confidently consider a 'good intention' under the umbrella of fantasy unless there is direct, consistent action to integrate that into a standard of living. If a good intention is only situational, it is not a standard but an exception. There is no place in standards for exceptions! That is devoid of the *entire* point.

Let's draw out a spectrum of standards playing inside of values. I don't intend to bestow my values or standards upon any of you, but if they sound intriguing, consider trying them and see how they alter the well-being and harmony in your life.

On Relationships

My partner never holding sex against me as a tool to inspire my change is a standard. Using my own desire to love her weaponized against me is not the healthy way to inspire me as the hero of our story. But how good the sex is remains a testament to how well we are doing as both individuals and as a harmonizing force. Something as good as sex should only be used as a celebration. Celebrate whatever you want, but please never weaponize somebody's desire for you. Alternatively, mutually coordinating it as a means of delayed gratification can help both of you prioritize your goals and then reward yourselves with one another. Double win! *Winky face.*

Not yelling in arguments is a standard. Consider this deeply from the guy writing a book about being pissed off. I do not hold a single memory where things got better when people thought screaming was a productive means of communicating. When it's standard, it means yelling is a problem that is so inefficient that it is below conduct I bother offering my time to. So, they agree to mellow and re-enter the conversation if they properly value me and the standard I hold. Or, I have to genuinely hold the line that I don't involve myself in situations where they operate in such a volatile manner.

If it repeats, it means I have to make more space between myself and that entire person's life. I can't see how that would be a loss if their manner of being violates my standard. That's how this works. The alignment amplifies harmony; anything that diminishes that has gotta go!

An aboriginal depiction of why people start to yell in disputes is not for lack of hearing but that our spirits have drifted far apart. Trust, self-composure, and gentle tones allow our spirits to come back and lean into one another. Extreme volume is only evidence of the disconnect.

You can create scales of 1-10 to illustrate a difference in standards within a shared value. Sure, me and my roommate both value cleanliness. So, let's build a scale of Cleanliness: 1 being a hoarder, and 10 being a clean freak. If my roommate's standard is 7-9 but mine is 6-8, then I may think their cleanliness at a 9 is overkill, while they think my cleanliness at 6 makes me a slob. It's better for me to raise my standards than to ask them to lower their standards for me. Everything suffers by submitting to the lower standard.

On Finances

The state of my finances is a standard. Not a 'Oh, I'd sure like this' but a factual state of how I live. At the beginning of the COVID-19 pandemic, when the world was a ghost town and all gyms were closed, I challenged myself to save as much money on food as possible. I, as a bachelor living alone, gave myself a $600 budget a month for my food. That's $20 a day. This was a time in my life when I had zero other crutches. I Spent nothing on video games, had a subscription to unlimited books, and did not indulge in alcohol, drugs, or anything else. Without having the gym to maximize my body's growth, I took a winter month to save as much on food as humanly possible to see what I'm made of. I think I ate 20-something cups of noodle soups. I only used $183 of the $600.

Just because I set the standard at $600 does not mean I need it. It's a ceiling. If I overstep, it means some other saving or standard has to suffer because I mismanaged the one I set in place. But too low is also simply detrimental to giving myself quality food. (I would never suggest anybody eat 20-something cups of noodles in a month. We all got a little weird during Covid.)

How much do I budget for play? How much do I budget for investing? Is that balance of play and growing appropriately stressing me? Or could I reach my goals sooner if I played less? I learned very quickly that zero play and all work diminish my productivity. My work suffers because I do not properly unwind. So, my version of play is a necessity to my balance. If I work hard, then playing and resting hard is also a standard for my well-being.

On the other side of finances, how little can I get down to before I lose my peace? When I can't focus on anything other than returning my relative idea of a safe amount of savings. Is it $30,000? $5,000? $500? Everybody's sense of financial security is relevant to what they've grown accustomed to. There is no right answer, only what we deem acceptable for ourselves. We can also decide to be appropriately frustrated with our financial state and consider our small budget an injustice to our potential. That frustration can be a healthy driving force to override the comfort that has become our plateau.

This is why people who live in poverty but win the lottery or are struck with an inheritance end up blowing their fortune. They have all excess but no sense of stress to set a new standard. Rather than considering a new standard to stabilize a higher state of being, their autopilot state of standards will have them return to their old normalcy. We have plenty of opportunities to redefine ourselves and elevate our standards. But that contentment with little can be an abundance killer if we aren't self-aware and intentional with the gifts we come across.

On Our Body

How your body looks is a standard. Sometimes, prolonged grieving, sickness or depression can have us exaggerating the use of our coping mechanisms. Whether it's under-eating, over-eating, or all other reactions to sorrow, the toll our body will inevitability manifest. We will summon the willpower to act at whatever point we look in the mirror and consider our physique an injustice to ourselves. When standardized, that anger of demanding better of yourself can be a safety mechanism. When anger at self is unhinged, it can amplify the self-defeating behaviours and neurologically create a new sense of self that stretches your standard lower. You may embody it if you look at yourself and call yourself pathetic. But if you look at yourself and recognize you have strayed from your magnificence, you will be inspired to return to it.

This means you have to define opportunities to prove your standard *amidst* your stress. If you stress-eat, then becoming aware and withholding from that urge is not self-denial, it is self-love. You either return to a self-respecting state or accept your diminished value as a natural consequence. Sorrow is a sinister bastard that way. It can last long enough to convince us that how we act just to survive is what we deserve rather than to inspire our continued pursuit of potential.

There are points when we may genuinely need an intervention and require the help of a friend or professional to recalibrate our standards and self-worth. There is absolutely no shame in needing assistance when we are dispirited or grieving. If we do not allow somebody of better sense to intervene, we'll continue to wallow and spiral downward within the behavioural byproduct of our sorrow.

The other side of the spectrum of exploring better health is an elevating journey. Seeing progress in the mirror and meeting versions of ourselves that we've never known inspires a sense of wonder about what the limit could be. It embeds the idea that if we work hard enough, we are capable of more.

This universal effort stretches across every standard. Holding the line to help people not yell is hard. Managing more finances than we've ever had is hard. Creating a body that can handle more than we've ever handled is hard. A 'good intention' accomplishes none of these things. The intention is only a primer for the actual action that becomes raw evidence of who we are or are not. The alternative to not setting our own standard is that everybody else decides our value, and we listen. If we don't declare our value, we will be forced to bargain with whatever others offer or declare for us.

On Bargaining with the Future

Your risk/reward tolerance is your standard of faith. The high end of your standard is how willing you are to dance with chance and shake up the routines in your universe. The low end of your standard is your reluctance to shift and leave lower-quality experiences behind for better ones. This standard seems backward because the high side of maintaining feels chaotic and unsure. But it is a means of playing and participating with the world. Whereas the low end is being on the defence of what the world is throwing at you. This is where divine anger calls upon you to realize you must play offensively to win points in any game. It expands your threshold upward.

Faith is an action word. Faith is radical action and confident patience. You'll find yourself saying, 'Well, we gave it a genuine effort!' You can find peace knowing something isn't 'meant to be' after a valiant effort. Maybe it's after fifty or one hundred valiant efforts. Then, you'll be content finding a new adventure, knowing the previous desire was thoroughly explored to fruition.

On the other hand, something might spark within you upon rejection of an even deeper desire to try again. But this time with experience! A few rejections may be redirections to something greater as you hone your talent. You set yourself apart as somebody who strives forward despite other's ability to see the value of what you're offering.

This standard of faith is the embodiment of your comfort zone. It is peace and clarity in the unseen. Emotional regulation, healthy finances and a healthy body are all things that will attract people who feel the same way, even if they haven't arrived yet. Alternatively, you will magnetize people who co-sign your unwillingness to grow. You will seek refuge in each other's complacent lifestyles.

Just as we lean on others to bounce back from losing health, wealth, or relational values, we can lean on others to navigate courageous action. You cannot gather courage from the advice of cowards. You cannot gather health from the advice of those who live unwell. You cannot learn love from people who cling to bitterness and operate by unmanaged emotions. It is easier to be somebody of epic faith among others who valiantly play with their potential in this life.

Momentum

Momentum is the most simple tool to understand your trajectory. What does one step lead to if followed through over a day or multiple years?

Cracking open one beer is not for one sip. It is for the whole can. So, it is not one act but 10-20 sips of momentum. If a beer is self-pleasure, you now have 10-20 acts of self-pleasure momentum. That momentum leads to a hundred more micro-gestures of self-pleasure in deeper intoxication. The drunk leads to the smoking that you swore off. Maybe even on to designer drugs. While you're at it, you might as well flirt with the people outside your relationship because the self-pleasing momentum is out of control. Now your integrous self has entirely left for the evening.

You might think you can get away with micro-gestures a few times until your tolerance builds. Then you need more to satisfy the same desire. You'll subtly get to more dangerous levels of the same game. It seems you just haven't paid a high enough price of consequences or hangover yet to hate the price of your pleasure. Maybe after you get a stranger pregnant, get a DUI or develop an addiction, you catch that 'maybe this isn't good for me.' But now bouncing back is not just stopping the initiating habit, it's entirely adapting your life around the stupid prize you won playing stupid games.

Alternatively, the momentum of cracking open a relationship book leads from one page to the next. It becomes a micro-gesture stacking of ideas that teach you to be a better lover and friend. After finding one tool that makes you more courageous, more humble, or better at conflict resolution, you wonder what other books offer. The micro-actions of reading page-after-page open shortcuts into skill sets that people have dedicated their entire lives to translating simply for your benefit.

That curiosity in mere minutes each evening stacked over multiple years now has the masterminded values of the world's best thinkers playing in your brain. In small effort, you rolled over into having substantially more wisdom, wealth and health than you previously did. You can't help but witness the overflow of what you've learned and shared with others now, bringing ease to their lives as well.

Momentum given to literally anything can't help but create results. It may take thirty minutes of procrastinating to pick up the guitar, but then ten minutes of plucking away each day leads to learning your 10 favourite songs within a year. The consequences of purposeful consistency are sexy. Any tiny effort stacked over one year will put you so far ahead of those not even trying. Realizing your own potential will very well literally scare you.

What *can't* you accomplish if you give it enough time? Any doubtful thought is merely self-sabotage, and anybody who loves you would honourably call you ridiculous for belittling yourself.

Perhaps the most realistic place to start is learning to interrupt yourself. Realizing you have any momentum in anything negative OR positive and practicing abrupt shifts proves you are always in control.

Are you driving? Take a new route home. Are you watching TV? Stop in the least convenient spot and shift to literally any other task. Are you eating or drinking something you said you wouldn't? Whip it in the garbage or pour it out without explaining yourself.

Practicing inconvenience is where the real power is at. Doing things when it makes sense isn't special. Practicing things when it feels the most inconvenient or opposed to your emotion is when you realize unequivocally you run this damn show. You are not a victim of desire on autopilot. You are a tiny God with unfathomable power to create new energy in your desired moment.

Oh Yea… I'm Pissed Off!

I'm amazed to ponder on this and realize how deep the mass psychosis runs for people to pawn a lack of integrity off as good intentions. I believe we are lenient because we wish others to be lenient and graceful with us. Although, grace for inaccuracy and challenging our well-being are two different things. The best circle of influence will elevate every standard we could possibly have. If anything, it would ideally be a constant game among friends and lovers to keep each other sharp and make light of the hard work that is improving ourselves.

Here is the big money question for this chapter: Do you find yourself more excited to outsmart and outmaneuver consequences and be an exception to rules? Or are you trying to blatantly do difficult things to achieve meaningful results for yourself and overflow to others?

Our tolerance of ourselves is what we validate for others around us. There is a constant energetic filtering at play in the universe. If people aren't sure if their bullshit will pass your standards, they will either see themselves out in advance or pressure-test your standards.

Why would you be in my life if you were more of a burden than a bonus? That is easy emotional math that children can handle. When did we lose that clarity? Oh ya, when we lost our clarity of self-worth. *Everything* stems from that idea and how you actually live it. Not how you *intend* to live it.

There is overflowing joy to be had in meaningful work and play alongside people you adore. We are all strange miracles from thousands of years of overcoming. Sooner or later, we all have to admit that humanity is merely built on the backs of our ancestors. Your 'best', no matter the definition, is the literal gift you offer humanity. It is impossible *not* to affect others we cross paths with. I'm not sure we have anything more important going on. Our best, or lack thereof, is embedded in every emotion we feel, every word we speak, and every step we take.

All the magic of life is in the minor details. How your spirit responds to difficulty and hardship is already predestined by the quality of standards you live out. When you squeeze the marrow out of life with your constant pursuit of maximizing the human experience, hell will have to find you in the little piece of Heaven that you've made for yourself.

There is no greater peace than in a person who meets the worst of the days knowing they did everything they could and took everybody they could with them. It's the worthiest battle we have.

Today's best pales compared to what our best will be in a week, month, or year. But that best is only built on the bricks of being that person today. When your best pays off, you can point at every daily brick laid as an undeniable stack of proof that our best efforts, flaws and all, are never in vain. It will prove itself in the love, peace, and trust you feel around you. All thanks to you becoming somebody who trusts themselves and lives out what they standardized. Others will be compelled to rise to that harmony or fall off and out of your life due to their own inconsistencies.

We are all in our right to call one another out on our inconsistencies. It's not rude. It's one of the most loving things we can do. If they don't like us exposing their own inconsistency and respond poorly, it means they are more committed to their inadequacy and inaction than they are to their relationship with you.

This is the direct road to hell - your own inability to lead yourself.

CHAPTER 15

Multi-Dimensionally Jacked

To fuck around is to be human. But to find out? That is divine.

My identity was a bit shaken after surviving more than three months off the grid as a Big Game Horseback Guide with my two brothers and fourteen horses. I handled standoffs with grizzlies, was swept down rivers chasing horses and even surrounded by wolves at one point. Some people react as if that makes me bold, but all that was obviously against my choice. I certainly became accustomed to it and learned to become incredibly comfortable in the wild, yet I was petrified to approach a girl in public. I gave myself incredible grief for feeling like a badass in one facet of my life, but a total coward compared to a much smaller challenge.

Not all courage is made equal. Somebody can be courageous in one area yet be stunned by other opportunities to be fully authentic. We may even compensate in our strength zones and consider ourselves having adequately risen to our occasions. Yet, how we refuse to show up will limit the wholeness of our potential. To embrace these various paths of courage is to become multi-dimensionally jacked. You will become an anomaly of character and ambition if you were to practice growth in all of these different facets of your life.

I've outlined six kinds of courage here to show the different atmospheres and expressions of bravery. The unbelievably cool thing about this is that practicing courage in one area of strength can amplify our courage in our weaker aspects. If we have talents and practice a physical form of courage, we can feel less anxious when similar nerves arise when attempting social courage. Or perhaps intellectual courage can cross over to amplify reasons to be hopeful when approaching a spiritual type of courage.

The great stack of proof you've made for yourself in rising to challenges breeds more opportunities for self-expression. There is no shame in starting small. Everybody's baseline comfort is entirely different. Wherever stress manifests is exactly where the growth does as well. However, the important note is that moderation is imperative in the spirit of sustained growth. After these six forms of courage that could double as a relationship enricher, I will explain two methods of building tolerance- exposure and rejection therapy. But for now, let's begin.

Physical Courage: To keep going with resilience, balance, and awareness.

This can be embodied in a multitude of ways. It can be defying fear by touching something we fear. It can be working past exhaustion in service to provide for the family. It can manifest in expanding our tolerance past our perceived limits. We have a sense of our bodily capability, whether it's how far we can jump, what we can lift, or what creature we can overpower or outmaneuver. It is one thing to assume we cannot succeed and entirely another liberation of self to find out and try anyway.

In another capacity, physical courage can mean sacrificing yourself for anything deemed worthy enough. It is to be the firefighter running into the burning building, the person who runs into traffic to catch the wandering pet, or the person who puts yourself in harm's way or endures pain on another's behalf. The tedious repetition can build a second nature of preparation against those who would do you or those you love harm. Even choosing a painful but possibly beneficial option, like undergoing chemotherapy, is courageous.

Social Courage: To be yourself unapologetically.

There is a difference between fitting in and truly belonging somewhere. Fitting in is having those finite conditions where people gather for cause or convenience on a common cord. True belonging is choosing to share space with somebody and be accepted entirely as you are, flaws and all. How much of yourself do you water down to remain in certain social circles? What parts of you are you deciding for others are not acceptable out of pure assumption?

I get it. Everybody is gauging comfort levels in social settings. You don't need that buffering period to be whoever you want. You'll either be respected or rejected. If they respect you, you're saving yourself time and fast-forwarding a positive relationship. If you are to be rejected, you realize where you clash with people that you were putting a facade up for. To what end?

We only feel strange and misunderstood in proportion to our ability to relate. I haven't met anyone I relate to on every note. But I've never needed somebody the exact same as me to feel understood. We crave others who are just caring, curious and enthusiastic about our well-being. Values will always determine who we align with, regardless of looks and quirky characteristics.

We all practice using the social lube of small talk. We dance around niceties and prod and offer each other bait for interesting conversation, wondering if the engagement will even be worth remembering. We keep applying social lube until there is an overflow of nothing, and it slips away. But if we are lucky, we catch actual traction and build engagement. But if we interact without intention, both sides are likely lukewarm and hoping the other offers the conversational foreplay.

The more excited we are about our own lives, the more that excitement overflows into our everyday interactions. Your own enthusiasm bursts out as the conversational foreplay to have something worth talking about. I've noticed most in my experience that people who are not proud or excited with how they spend their free time are most averse to diving into how they are *actually* doing. They resort to shallow autopilot small talk.

Using myself as an example, I hated the idea of admitting I spent an entire weekend playing video games. Not to say video games are bad, but I self-imposed my guilt and shame on my pastime because I apparently had a facade of productivity to portray. So, I would dance around the reality and say my weekend was 'relaxing' while not actually being very relaxed about reflecting on my own use of my time. But if I accomplished any remote amount of a task or adventure, I'd express the highlights to build my sense of character and ambition to others. It had nothing to do with what the other thought, but I clearly didn't think highly of my own use of time, whether I enjoyed it or not. I acted inauthentic to my company, limiting their ability to be true friends and know me for who I am.

Maybe we were playing the same games and could have shared excitement. Maybe they would ask if I got any writing done and hold me accountable to my own sense of urgency. They *care* about my accomplishments, just like I do for them. I'll never know whether they would shame me or not, but I decided they would *for* them. The worst-case fear of not being accepted manifested by default by not accepting *myself* in the first place. I acted as if their shame towards me was already a fact. All of this out of "How was your weekend?" This is how wild our brains really go behind the scenes.

I have a beckoning built into myself, navigating and narrating my own sense of worth. Whether I walk that line allows me to move with clarity, peace, and conviction of my own capability. If compelled, I can re-evaluate and reform that internal compass whenever I please and entirely change my life's mission. But other people - if they are to care about me to any degree of depth - need me to be able to express who I am and where I am going if they are to help me walk tall.

On the other hand, I need to help those I care for to be able to articulate their own sense of self and direction if I am to help hold them high. I need them to be strong enough to be honest to have a quality connection and be sounding boards of value for each other. This is how we stop feeling alone in a room full of people. Especially when we find ourselves not proud of our lifestyle. There is no shame in needing a hand to crawl out of a chasm of our own digging behind closed doors. Being too prideful to receive help is the true enemy in this scenario.

Courage is a two-way street when we notice the quickness to irritation, the mail piling up, the lack of stillness, and whatever other telltale signs of distress. I need courage to hold space and embody grace for somebody who is not giving grace to themselves, just as much as I need to give that to myself. It should never be a scary or rude space to ask if somebody is not being all they can be. We should be able to make that case for ourselves at any and all times. What else are we doing if not being intentional? Auto-pilot is synonymous with handing the power away. If we are not entirely captivating our own lives, something else is captivating and capitalizing on us.

Moral Courage: Doing the right thing even when uncomfortable or unpopular.

There is something called 'The shopping cart morality test.' It tests whether somebody returns a shopping cart to an orderly, convenient place for the store workers or stalls. Each degree of orderliness could theoretically reveal a subconscious moral ethic of somebody's character.

It is not illegal to leave a shopping cart somewhere inconvenient, so there is (seemingly) no backlash for it. It is to assume somebody will pick up after you - though they will - and that your few seconds to put the shopping cart away are more valuable than the shop workers.

This *Dungeons and Dragons-style* morality test is a widely shared internet meme and is summarized like this:

Lawful Good: Returned cart to the store.

Chaotic Good: Launching a cart into a cart corral.

Lawful Neutral: Returned cart to a *different* store.

Chaotic Neutral: Returned cart to nature.

Lawful Evil: Neatly stacked carts somewhere inconvenient.

Neutral Evil: Left cart in parking spot.

Chaotic Evil: Tossed cart into ditch.

See how many layers there are to a trivial act of society? The essence of moral courage is sacrificing something of self for the greater good. Or at least the *assumption* that somebody's day is better or easier since you noticed a way that it could be helped.

If you have a moment to be of any measure of service to the world, do you make it a priority in your day? Or, on the deeply courageous side, what are you doing to disrupt the corruption and chaos in your atmosphere?

Spiritual Courage: Living with purpose and meaning through a heart-centred approach towards all life and oneself.

Spirituality and morality can be interlinked, but I'll draw a separation for clarity. If morality is a relationship with your sense of the greater good, then spirituality is a relationship with your purpose, placement and personal meaning that *you* give life. It makes sense that if you have a trajectory and perspective of life, consequences, and what happens after you die, you can mingle that with morality. But that spirituality holds a space between who you are and a belief of what is harmony in the culture and eternity. The closer we feel 'grounded' to our spiritual self, the more peace and contentment we seem to have with the unfolding of our lives.

"For God is not the author of confusion, but of peace."[iv] - 1 Corinthians 14:33

Spirituality is aligning a life direction that justifies your actions toward yourself and others as a meaningful purpose. Integrity is to be whole, to have all facets of your life in concordance with your values and harmony with the whole.

As all other forms of courage have a root of rationale to overcome a barrier, spiritual courage is far more absurd. Spiritual courage can be to pay close attention to the things we can't help but fixate on. Spiritual courage is nourishing ourselves in a way that we prioritize creativity. Whether it be a dedication to crafts like music, art, building or adventure. It is where the act itself is entirely captivating for the sake of its own quality. Spiritual courage is not knowing where a path leads, but the beckoning of the experience is enough. No matter where it takes us.

It may begin with a goal, but the *journey* is a spiritual experience. It's our ability to recognize that each step of the way is worthwhile. Whether we hate it or love it. Whether it breaks our spirit or makes us cry happy tears. It is the build-up, the anticipation, and the character creation along the way that the end goal can represent. The goal was just an idea to move towards, but all we become in character is spiritual development.

I'm not painting this with vibrant colours as I know true courageous journeys can lead to agony and resentment. Courage from that point of pain is the will to carry on without being embittered by your experiences. We cannot let the end of one story dictate the assumption of how all other courageous attempts will unfold for us. Whether in business, life or love.

The consequences are the aftermath of a journey thoroughly ventured. Some journeys are cut short for their own reasons, but the sake that we start is the calling we must answer. It's a radical acceptance that choosing something means sacrificing something else.

We can't have it all. But we can give ourselves the peace of our own life being thoroughly used up. It's hard to be anxious when you know you've shown up for a day with everything your body, mind and soul could muster. It will feel like no matter what happens, the universe has a proper order, and we played the finest part we could offer.

Monotony breeds discontent in our spiritual selves. Something inside of us knows there is more to life than what we are currently experiencing. How will you go forth and tickle that intuitive itch that has been gifted to you?

Intellectual Courage: Learning, unlearning, and relearning with an open and flexible mind.

That which knows how to bend will not break. Bending is not just surrendering to pressure but attuning and adapting. If you stand by your ideals in the spirit to belittle other's ideals, healthy debates are rarely possible. Conversations and sharing thoughts or ideas were never meant to be a dangerous activity. If we are rigid in our thinking, we see conflicts and problems all around us. If we are playful and curious in our character to understand the world, every conversation is an opportunity.

Even science is the practice of 'the truth for now.' Strong opinions loosely held are greater for humanity than loose opinions strongly held. We can be fooled by pure, unbridled confidence, so be aware of the facade of convictions. Are people speaking from lived proof or just passionate pride?

Humility is usually a good sign that somebody has really done their due diligence. Much of humanity is desperate and funnels to the path of least resistance. We fall into ruts of communal agreement for safety and simplicity's sake. The price of communal bias is your free will to think and challenge ideas.

If you cannot form a rational possibility that, if presented, could change your ideology, then be weary of blindly following a thought with religious immunity. Like a sacred text which makes all others inferior for not agreeing or involving themselves. Intellectual strictness can border on delusion and ego inflation.

If people trust each other's capacity to find a life that fits their values, every curiosity is fair game. Almost all knowledge can be passed down (and *should* be) to ease us through the infinite options of this life. But you must also walk into the same murky waters that others do to grow your own experiential convictions. It's like reading the description of how a meal tastes but never savouring the flavour yourself.

You are not just a messenger of other people's hearsay and stories. You have your entirely own unique story to craft and speak from. Others may influence, inspire, and teach you so much, but at the end of the day, you are a unique expression of intelligence waiting to witness the world for itself.

Ask the questions that scare you. Ask why things are taboo. Ask why people are as they are. When you realize the answer is never simple or rarely two of the same, you will see an intellectual journey waiting around every corner.

Emotional Courage: Feeling all your emotions without guilt or attachment. Both good and bad.

To reiterate this concept, all emotional pain is a form of separation. separation from self, from a sense of worth, from reality, from others, from purpose, from ideal, from convenience.

Giving yourself space to be a spectator of your own emotions is one of the most powerful skills to practice. It's very primal to hear bad news and want to scream, cry, reach for that swig of whiskey, run away, etc. If we take a moment to still ourselves before our body carries us to those ways of reacting, we can instead choose a response. Against all our urges, this is where we have an opportunity to express and master our energy in motion.

Our emotional programming is like being a rider atop an elephant. It is not a rejection of your emotions and instinct to stop yourself - the elephant - before responding. It is an opportunity to validate your instinct but choose a more productive or less harmful means of guiding yourself. When we are not calculated, we receive pain and transmit it through ourselves as well. Alternatively, we can receive, feel, and hold that feeling long enough to transmute it into something beautiful.

Of course, that pertains to the negatives. Yet, we can have blind spots in our ecstatic joys as well. I am all for amplifying joys, but there is a way to calculate and project that energy in a healthy way. Be careful not to boast of good luck or success to the masses. Instead, share with people who have a vested interest in your well-being. Your rising tide raises their ships, even if it's only in spirit. Flaunting to those who do not celebrate your victories may create a spotlight for people to channel their resentments and self-dissatisfaction.

If negative sensations are to be chaotic, it only makes sense that joy could also be chaotic. We can have a sense of achievement and feel like we deserve rest. But there is a saying that if you want to kill a crocodile, you must attack it once its belly is full. When satiated, its ambition is tainted and is nearly paralyzed in its satisfaction.

Be careful not to dull your ambitions, ethics, and momentum in a feasting season. Do not take one burst of success and lose touch with hard and meaningful work. Normalizing a new state of abundance leaves you vulnerable to losing something that is only a bonus to your life experience. Remember that you were once sustained, well, and satiated by less. Your emotions can bond to a temporary bliss and call it loss when the time has passed. Not all separation is loss. It can be a redirection. A time for planning. A time to be open to new beginnings.

Exposure Therapy

It doesn't matter if you're afraid of spiders, dogs, belly buttons, public speaking, elevators, or being watched by a duck. All fear has a threshold of tolerance that we can play with.

Nomophobia, the fear of being without a mobile phone or cellphone coverage, may already be weighing on our current and future generations. This is another opportunity to optimally challenge ourselves, no matter where our personal starting point takes us. Exposure therapy is a simple and calculated tactic for conquering these anxieties.

Exposure therapy is a type of behavioural therapy that involves gradually exposing an individual to a feared object, situation, or activity in a safe and controlled environment. The goal is to reduce anxiety or fear associated with the trigger.

For example, if someone fears spiders, they may start exposure therapy by looking at pictures of spiders. Then, gradually progress to being in the same room as a spider in a jar. In progression, eventually touching a spider while under the guidance and supervision of a therapist. The exposure is designed to help the individual become more comfortable with the feared object or situation and learn to cope with their anxiety or fear response. This approach can be effective in treating various anxiety disorders, phobias, and PTSD.

The warning necessary for this is that a controlled environment is initially essential. The whole point of fear is in moments without control, though small progressions must be under the participant's own willingness. It is the way that pain and trauma are bestowed upon us without consent that leaves such a profound mark. If an exposure therapy session gets out of hand and pushes the participant's threshold, the effort may backfire as a deepened insecurity and powerlessness.

Fear is inherently the sensation of feeling 'unsafe' even if you are. Imagine that if you can create your own safety, you can empower others just the same. Whether you outwit or overpower it, your becoming is proof that it is possible for others. Once again, your diligence may become others' deliverance.

In the spirit of previous chapters suggesting we cannot do this alone, welcoming a friend into this exposure therapy process can become an incredible bonding experience. If you want to deepen a friendship quickly, conquer fears with them. You will associate ecstatic overcoming and courage with their presence. You can build a momentum of overcoming and adventure with people you welcome into this typically timid nook of your personality.

To reiterate nomophobia, the fear of being without a mobile phone or cellphone coverage is evidently an adaptive anxiety that wasn't even a concept until 1973. All life prior-to was not inferior or riddled with this terror. The normalcy was that we walked out into the world and had to be alright without a virtual hand always in reach. That is now something we must diligently make time for to return to the basic state of courage demanded of the human experience. Our opportunity to set ourselves aside and be extraordinary in the eyes of our average society is available in every waking moment. Our emotions and anxieties are a playground, not a fact of limit.

Rejection Therapy

Sometimes, it helps to crank up the dose of what we fear to a depersonalizing level. Asking for one person's number feels like a monumental win or loss waiting to happen. But asking for fifty phone numbers in one day takes the pressure off each individual instance. The goal is to learn from your results rather than wallow in each instance. You have forty-nine more numbers to ask for.

The curiosity can override the fear. Your skillset naturally grows in the process. My personal 'rejection' therapy was in creating social media content. I had an adversity to being on camera and was overly critical of myself. But I believe the things I'm fascinated by would also fascinate others. Regardless of how I'm judging myself, I think the value I'm sharing transcends whatever bullshit is in my own way.

Instead of being overcritical of the performance and how each short video is perceived, I decided to make a hundred short videos per year. I didn't go viral until around video 230, when half a million people agreed to be sick of boring-ass conversations. Thus, my introspection and relationship-building book, *Compass of Connection*, was born.

That one-minute video opened up a slew of opportunities. I now had an entire library of content for people to browse and enrich themselves with. The previous 230 videos weren't necessarily inferior but stepping stones to a refined way of speaking. My curiosity about how psychological information can help others overpowered the anxiousness of being on camera. Whether I get to witness the results or not, it always slaps back in fascinating ways.

Whatever value you truly put higher will win.

Integrity

Mastering the fears that wall away different facets of your experience may be your life's hardest yet most rewarding challenge. By rationalizing hardships and amplifying the smallest joys, you can become somebody who orchestrates your own life's sensations. This makes you a significant asset to any relationship, team, or mission you could ever be a part of.

You are the only person who can validate your own courageousness. Others may relate to your struggle or sympathize, but the experience and choices are yours. It is scary and wonderful that nobody else can shoulder your courageous battles for you. Even if somebody accomplishes a task that scares you, you are not relinquished from fear as it will pass on to the next opportunity. That is why it is essential to rise to an occasion as it presents itself. Otherwise, an old familiar terror may slowly grow more daunting.

It's like walking to a waterfall and being blocked outside the destination by a bridge. Others effortlessly walk by and prove it's a secure bridge. The view below sucks the air right out of your lungs, even though there is a railing to aid you. You watch as the other people ahead are struck with awe at the waterfall, yet you remain behind the bridge. Either you commit to becoming somebody who can rationalize your security, or you surrender the waterfall as an experience that only others deserve. The world was not made smaller or diminished, but *yours* was. Life is as rich as you are courageous.

If you cannot find a way to make peace with the challenge not taken or the risk not ventured, then you also risk resenting those who do. A great indicator of somebody's lack of self-esteem is how freely they belittle other's ambitions. Anybody who understands worthwhile adventures can grow the emotional capacity to wish others well in their ambitions.

This takes us back to the spiritual portion of courage. The clarity brings peace that no matter how bizarre or trivial somebody else's desires are, they will face their own consequences and be sorted by the universe accordingly. If you genuinely play your edge and expand your potential, you will be too busy to waste time speaking poorly of others. Discovering your own potential is an all-encompassing life task.

As a final note for this chapter, we all know it's an inevitable feature of the human experience to have another human doubt us, especially somebody we consider 'close' to us.

"Mama said that a h-a-t-e-r is just a person with their h-e-a-r-t all jumbled up." - Pages Matam.[v]

Have compassion for haters. They must have spent so long behind that bridge, watching others reach the waterfall and feeling sorry for themselves. Their discontent was deep in their own life before you ever provoked them. People who belittle other's genuine ambitions are quietly crying for help to have a more interesting life than the one they've given themselves. We all know that this big world has many unfathomable pleasures. You must be profoundly disturbed to hope somebody else's sunshine is dimmed in your time of darkness.

Fear makes courage *necessary*. It takes courage to move in the unknown with the belief we won't die. Courage is the extension of our hand to the future, a gamble with the universe that we can be all the better for. It's the most foundational game we can play.

If the granddaddy of all questions is, "Is life worth living?" Courage is your response: "I'll find out for myself."

Chapter 16

Perfection

I bet everybody at one point farted a little by accident when they sneezed. People's attempt to act perfect is just insecurity with lipstick on. Grow up and let the child in you enjoy the 'whoopsies' of life again. Stop shaming each other for being human, and learn to laugh at how silly this life is.

I promise humour trumps perfectionism around every corner. Perfectionism isolates you as somebody nobody can relate to since it's an unobtainable ideal. Meanwhile, humour finds lightheartedness in all seriousness. I can't wait for my crow's feet to be deep and obvious so you can see I lived long and laughed plenty.

The ideal of perfection is that something can't get any better. Taking a person in totality and saying, 'This is as good as they will ever get,' might be more of an insult than anything. It would be quite defeating if you could be sure that you've already passed the peak of your life and everything would be less-than from there forward.

The fact that we can never know is a good reason to keep living. I have felt some exquisite joys in my twenty-seven years, but there are so many yet to stumble into. So many more people who will blow my paradigm of possibility wide open. The reality of endless growth and refinement is what keeps us fresh, on our edge, and eager for every new day's potential.

Perfection more closely embodies insecurity as a characteristic. Which, I quite enjoy that irony. It should insinuate an entire lack of insecurity, but rather is an obsessive compensation of them. Attempting perfectionism is a clear act of disconnection. It's surrendering your power to other's approval.

As I have suffered from the impossible pursuit myself, I understand it is rooted in a desire for acceptance and a sense of accomplishment. It shook my tree when I realized that there is a significant difference between being valuable and being valued. Being valuable is a measure of performance. Being valued is to be cherished in the absence of performance. What a slippery slope justifying our existence through performance has become.

An Ideal State

Let's pretend you have - just for this moment - made peace with your insecurities on just one of the things you aspire to do. You would be intrinsically motivated, meaning your own free will, curiosity, pleasure, development, and passion for that goal drive you. No external pressure or threat is involved in your relationship with this craft.

Take piano, for example. You might be curious about the power of song and how it can summon and enrich the experience for people around you. The learning process always brings you one step closer to expanding your potential to deliver something you believe serves a magnitude of joy to the world. How your fingers fall and sometimes fumble into the wrong keys makes you laugh, not furious. You treat it like a language you're learning rather than a performance to be judged. Now, you are not just imitating art before you, but rather finding a unique expression of your pleasure for others to hear and feel. What was once mere interest is now a craft that makes strangers and loved ones bob their heads in coffee shops and shopping malls.

You interrupted existence itself and enriched the collective experience.

There was no looming threat to your well-being to be at a certain skill at a certain time. Your finances were not at risk if your fingers were to slip. Moreover, you did not belittle *yourself* for fumbling mid-performance. Your perseverance now adds magnitude as people noticed your sheer passionate endurance. You use this craft as a playground of your courage and surrender to how the universe will respond to your skills with admiration and opportunity. In that unknowing response to our expression, a story-worthy life can unfold in its purest form. It is a story born of sheer intuition and self-driven passion.

Nobody's jealousy of the attention you receive could belittle your expression. You understand there is greater skill out there than you. But you are not in competition. You are in collaboration with the human experience. Your unique expression gives others permission to be seen, heard and expressed.

Comparison is disastrous, while competition is divine. Comparison diminishes people in a spirit of silent judgment. Meanwhile, competition forms like love, fueling the flame of what is possible as people sharpen their talent against and alongside one another. Competition works the same magic, whether in the spirit of play or professionalism.

The inevitable judgment and 'haters' who may try to stifle your flame are simply feedback. A dishonest acquaintance that only ever says 'sounds good' is not near as valuable as the feedback of somebody's honest thought that 'that part didn't make sense'. Distaste is also constructive feedback if you know how to receive it properly. Even those who wish your downfall are conspiring in your favour if you twist their input into fixing your blind spots. This is the spirit of anti-fragility. Perfectionism could never cast a shadow on the magnitude of somebody open and willing to receive all forms of feedback as a means to better themselves.

With this intrinsically motivated approach to our craft, we give ourselves permission to celebrate the fingerprint of our expression—flaws and all. Perfection could never share any of the above lessons with those before us. Perfection doesn't offer the feedback loop that comes with consistent trial and error. Perfection fears anything other than positive feedback. Perfection limits human connection.

What greater foul could we normalize to society than belittling the enthusiastic fumbling it takes to grow as human beings? It's literally our universal experience as children growing up. But somehow, we bought into the 'mistakes are fatal' mindset. It has inspired so much fear that the vast majority of society has entirely stifled their self-expression as a result.

If you want to wage war on perfectionism, study intrinsic motivation. Start to experiment with what brings out your progressive curiosity and joyfully challenges your skillsets. It is not realistic for something that genuinely challenges you to never frustrate you, but striving itself feels like a worthwhile way to exhaust your energy. The ultimate difference is that intrinsic motivation feels like spiritual play.

We cannot outwork people who treat their craft like play. People who don't require external rewards like a paycheck, validation or praise to keep working will sustain unparalleled momentum. People who are joyful in their craft are more capable of creative thinking. This means the 'win' isn't just a job well done. It's the freedom to play with all the elements of the craft and redefine the definition of 'winning' entirely.

Perfection cannot fathom the freedom and playfulness required to inspire innovation. The ability to go astray and mingle outside the rules has brought forth the future. The future truly belongs to those who experiment with the spirit of intelligent play, like nothing but *grown-up children*. So, this is a statement for you to *grow up* and bring your childlike curiosity and enthusiasm back to life.

Anti-Illusion

We are doing our best with all of life's information we've accumulated to evaluate our self-worth. Optimizing opportunity and minimizing rejection is everybody's ambition to one degree or another in relation to their goals. Much of the world participates in illusory tactics to meet their desired ends. Let me share a mishap of mine before hopping into the grit of the illusions we take part in.

I've ordered various skincare products online, as I've battled a rosy, dry complexion for most of my life. I've been loyal to a brand for quite a while until they did some rebranding and temporarily stopped the specific lotion I used. I tried to order the next closest thing, which doubled as sunscreen.

Sounds great! It also said something about colour or tone correction but didn't blatantly say 'foundation' on it. So, when I put it on, I start smearing this tone all over my face, thinking it will rub in, but it's clearly makeup. For a few minutes, my face was all one healthy-looking tone, and let me tell ya, I looked *good*. It was slightly cakey since my face was already dry, and I had no idea what I was doing. But for a minute, I realized how powerful and sexy all you women must feel when you transform your natural tone into whatever work of art you choose for the day.

In comparison to generational industries mastering the art of subconscious attraction, a natural face can hardly compete. Here is where I say that I'm not anti-beauty; I'm anti-illusion. We are all literally art in human form already. We only amplify our creativity and magnificence with what we can do. But we chase a slew of false idols of perfection, making us feel less divine every day that we compare ourselves.

What is absolute nonsense is that we draw some of our inadequacy from not yet outsmarting human biology and making ourselves Barbie and Ken dolls. We are way too interesting, miraculous, and unique to make that an actual normalcy. The propaganda is so thick that it's now seen as revolutionary boldness for a woman to be in public or at work without putting on a mask. It's as if our natural form has been declared lesser-than and vulnerable.

Ladies and gentlemen, you cannot monetize human decency. But you can monetize reality-altering and reality-amplifying art. Who cares if it shatters women's ability to embrace their own naked faces? Who cares if men are so normalized to expecting an unrealistic standard that they lose touch with embracing a woman's natural state?

Not the industry.

We can't monetize sheer ambition and dedication, but you can monetize performance enhancements and body modifications. Who cares if they manipulate users' chemical composition and make them emotionally unstable?

Not the industry.

You can't monetize charisma and confidence. But you can monetize the social lubricant of drugs and alcohol. Who cares if it's a minor poison to our motor skills and reasoning if it means we get pseudo-courage? Who cares if it becomes so normal that people aren't sure if it's the sober or drunk version who is more honest? Who cares if it becomes an addictive crutch to cope with reality?

Not the industry.

So! I'm pissed off that being disconnected from reality is so far normalized that trying to amplify reality makes *me* the outlier. The people with something to sell just found a way to romanticize their product by subtly insulting you.

You could be beautiful!
You could be strong!
You could be courageous!

Make sure you don't miss how your fundamental essence is being belittled in the sales pitch. You can't suggest a superior aesthetic, physique, or state of being without suggesting the current state is inferior. And you wouldn't buy it unless you agreed.

I'm pissed off that when I tell somebody that they are beautiful, they flinch because they aren't sure if I'm talking to them as a whole or the mask that they put on. When you aren't authentic, you can't be sure which parts people say they admire. You've already predetermined your unlovable part. You've written off the possibility people could adore you despite those parts you haven't made peace with yet.

I'm pissed off that natural physical growth has been allowed to pale in comparison to body-mangling 'enhancements.' The conversation of health is secondary to aesthetics because so many are surrendering their worth to the admiration of others.

I'm pissed off that sober inadequacy is so rampant and silently suffered that many people's sustained aspiration is to escape reality. For that reason, some are also no longer here. It's literally written into the language, 'wasted.' Not enlightened. Not empowered. *Wasted.*

I'm pissed off that it's normalized that happiness and fulfillment are now pursued through artificial means. We've fallen so far from basic satisfaction, fulfillment and connection that we sell serotonin in a capsule. I'm pissed off that compensating is so normal that being human is becoming outdated, and we are falling more and more in lust with our compensated and medicated identity.

We must then fall asleep with the version of us we are afraid to show every night. It's no wonder we feel lost and lack a sense of wholeness. We've tortured our own genius to conform in such measly ways that even we know in the core of our being that we have undone ourselves. We are too far gone to simply state that we feel like fucking frauds and start reconciling with who we *really* want to be.

We desperately need to look at each other - blemished parts and all - and remind each other that we have untapped potential that the universe is begging to witness. I promise when you stop watering down what you really have to say and what you're passionate about, you find a momentum that nobody's mopey-ass attitude and lack of self-love can stop.

Somebody once spoke life into me when I had nothing to offer them. That's when I knew they weren't lying. I hope you feel the same way here. I will remain obsessed with paying that blessing forward until the day I die. In that, I captivate my anger despite the years I was pleasing the wrong people for the wrong reasons to feel less alone. That priceless suggestion that I had value embedded in me by default renewed my ability to be well again and serve others.

No monetary exchange was needed. Only a sincere recognition of a perfectly imperfect person with an entire life ahead of me to redesign as I deem fit. It was the equivalent of a spiritual defibrillator to shock me out of my own bullshit and be reminded the best is yet to come if I only got out of my own way.

Intimacy

That sensation of loneliness that amplifies as we build our facade is a crooked feeling. Loneliness is a feeling that, despite the presence of others, nobody 'sees' us. But how can somebody 'see' us in any true sense if who we've presented to them is just a sales pitch of what we assume they will like? I reiterate that fitting in is having to mould ourselves to blend in, whereas belonging is being accepted while being entirely ourselves. Zero compromises of character and being, flaws and all. Trying to 'fit in' might be a direct route to losing our sense of self if we aren't careful.

Mankind's insecurity crafted perfectionism, but humanity was crafted by something far more profound. Therefore, perfectionism is already sub-par to the truth of humanity. We must learn to celebrate each other's true natures and vulnerability. Otherwise, our connection becomes artificial. Our wounded parts, quirks, and strangeness must be embraced for us to be truly human. The attempt to act above or better than humanity brings such agony to our spirits. If we fall out of tune with ourselves, we lose tune with all others.

If you have the audacity to be wholly human, you can experience true intimacy. Intimacy is not exclusively romantic, but to be loved and appreciated as you are. If you are busy painting a false reality of who you are, people will fall in love with a ghost you've given them and wonder why you feel none of that connection. They will argue that they know you while you feel it in your gut that they aren't even close. Yet, you are the one who led them to that misunderstanding.

This sensation arises when we know in our core that we are not being authentic. The price of trying to live that falsehood and never knowing true intimacy would breed the ultimate failure of resenting love. Being so bitter as to belittle another's love for one another is the most obvious representation of our resentment of ourselves. Ironically, only love can heal that wound.

Be yourself. So that people who are looking for you can find you.

Chapter 17

Befriend the Monster

I sat on this chapter for two whole years more than any other. Something about its original version called 'Manage the Monster' initially gave me a sense of pride, but rereading it felt like a genuine insult to myself. I couldn't put my finger on why.

I knew I was consciously calling what I considered my character defects to be of a monstrous quality. Why? It gave me something to fight. I was using coping mechanisms and acting outside of my integrity by self-soothing. I was operating out of fear and insecurity. I considered anything that split my integrity to be 'the enemy.' But allow me to express what happens when you claim a part of yourself and your unmet needs as the 'enemy.'

What does somebody do when they are too afraid of what they are facing? Our instinct is to destroy or run from it. So, when you become afraid and feel you cannot trust yourself, the mix of running from or attempting to destroy yourself manifests as poorly as it sounds. And what do monsters do? They terrorize and destroy. I felt - despite the piling admirable qualities I've dedicated my entire adulthood to building - I had a part of me I needed to destroy.

This chapter is a testament to self-forgiveness.

Meet the Monster

We commonly communicate our character defects and bad habits as 'demons.' But sometimes, it takes a demon to expose the truth.

Maybe you're like me and need tough love. The 'You can do whatever you set your mind to, honey!' doesn't strike me like, 'You know this secret habit you're dancing around is the reason you don't respect yourself, right?'

The thing is, I know I can do it, *honey*. But sometimes, I think I can stay committed to my old bullshit comfort habits that steal time from my best myself, and I wonder what I can get away with. We are all our own ultimate adversaries. I wholly believe no man nor woman can tear me down even a shred compared to the damages I can do unto myself. That is why I have so much respect and compassion for those battling addiction. This comes back to disease resulting from a failed harmonizing to our life. How we cope and self-soothe with that disharmony comes in all forms of disheartened spirits and troubled minds.

As we progress in our self-development, we don't slay our demons; we befriend them and hear their stories.

Those old ways of ours don't die. We validate their role in trying to distract or suppress an agony that boils beneath our awareness. We come to intimately understand what, where, when, and why it came to be a way we cope with the chaos we could not outrun or drown out. The 'demons' or less-admirable qualities we have are still all *us*. We cannot slay the monster if it is us. We forgive which part of us *has* monstrous capacity. We captivate it. We console it. We master it.

It is said the opposite of addiction is not sobriety; it is connection. Some sides of us are not conquered with sheer self-will but with human connection and love. When you are the enemy, you need something and somebody outside of you to remind and instill that you are worth redemption. When something is sick inside of us, we need antibiotics. That means we have micro-organisms that are strategically used to go in and annihilate what is doing us ill. Some battles are simply ridiculous to fight alone.

When that war is you against yourself and you don't know who to trust, you need humility to allow somebody else to guide you when your intuition has gone astray. You will have to separate from the part that thinks you're too good for help. Love is that controlled burn that dissolves the ego and pride as you, like a forest, grew anew from the ashes.

In spirituality, we wage war on our own vices with virtues. Meet anybody with a spiritual story, they will say any higher power (of their own unique understanding) pulled something better out of them. They might have had some form of transfiguring event - usually a rock bottom - to contemplate that something so far beyond us is not only real but has a vested interest in us. Grace amid those darkest days is what we can offer one another. How unbelievable that when we have every reason to convince one another that we are unlovable and unworthy of grace, grace and patience will be what saves us anyway.

I have no spiritual agenda here; you will all sort yourselves out. I trust you can handle a bit of spiritual ramble without getting your feathers ruffled and hopefully gain from my angle of it. Even if you think you believe in nothing, whatever your relationship is with your own death *is* your spirituality. Whatever your highest value is that filters all your decisions may be your god. That relationship to death and your value towards life builds your mental guardrails of your worth and your sense of eternity or lack thereof. Whatever you think of yourself is the umbrella of limitations you imagine for every other person, too. You can't say your life is worthless and convince somebody else that theirs is valuable. Other people are the exact same amount of a miraculous accident in space and time as you are.

Your idea of value governs your vision, so I hope you didn't choose a pessimistic lens to spend your whole life wearing. Happy people avoid pessimism like the plague... And as Covid-19 has proven, even an over-exaggerated plague is still a pain in our ass no matter how hard we avoid it.

There is that saying that we are 'made in God's image.' So we are either in constant pursuit of being in touch with a higher power, or you've written off the possibility entirely. That pursuit towards a 'God-given potential' allows people to believe it and achieve it, whereas non-believers of anything can justify it every which way, like 'They had it in them all this time. It has nothing to do with any God.'

Well, *even if* you're correct, that makes two possibilities. For one, that makes *them* part-God, and you are agreeing to your inferiority. *Or*, you're just as magical and capable of drawing solutions out of thin air as the rest of us accidental miracles. Why are people so committed to their inadequacy to justify their victimhood and passivity to their own healing?

My God and my ultimate pursuit is the expansion of love, adventure and potential. Studying and maximizing gratitude year over year directed that I build fulfillment on those fundamental forms of inner richness. When I embody those three things, I can magnify that in the world. Anything that might feel incredible but diminishes those qualities is my self-proclaimed nemesis. However, it is a proper and powerful adversary to have created for myself. Let me explain.

My Stupid Game and My Stupid Prizes

After writing my life story, *'An Arsenal of Gratitude,'* I realized what a mountain of *inefficiencies* this life handed me. Inefficient again, synonymous with stupid, so I can safely diagnose my own stupidity with how tumultuous my life was before all the self-reflection and intentionality. Using the magic of language, I can call out very sensitive topics, replace 'stupid' with 'inefficient', and make what I say perfectly agreeable.

An example is saying that having an addiction is inefficient when trying to build a balanced lifestyle. But if I say addiction is stupid, even though I'm not wrong, 'stupid' is an emotionally charged word of shame. Calling addiction stupid would be disregarding those born addicted from mothers amid drug abuse, those never taught any healthy coping mechanisms, those escaping trauma or PTSD, and so many other compassionate situations not to be a jackass about. So, when faced with my own obliviousness to the consequences of pornography, my self-righteousness imploded. My holier-than-thou complex was humbled. I was put in my place with the recklessness of my shame that manifested shortly after.

I don't think I had any outstanding justifications for my obliviousness or the lack of intrigue for the consequences of addiction, which, in my case, was pornography. I could blame the culture and the 90% of other boys since the age of 12 who were in the same boat to varying degrees. If anything, the topic was humorous and refraining from using porn made you the weird one. As if those who didn't use it were missing out on different flavours that the universe was offering at supposed 'no cost.'

After the broad consequences of relational insecurity, practiced secrets and lack of self-control were brought to light, I had no choice but to face the reality and *choose* my inefficiency from that point forward. With the level of ambition, integrity and calibre of lifestyle I was fighting to uphold, I had to seek my internal depths of why this craving had such a hold on me. I thought I could outsmart my own weakness rather than conquer it like the real divine masculine I was attempting to embody as cheaply and as short-cut as possible. Which is entirely opposed to the point, isn't it?

I frame the importance of my sexual energy like this. If my essence has enough power to literally incubate life, that is the definition of the potential for life. If I surrender that pure potential to pixels on a screen, my biology might be *convinced* of a great victory of intimacy, but my soul will be cheated of a real connection. If an act designed for intimacy and connection is twisted into an isolated practice, I figure it is an appropriate consequence when it manifests as dreadful loneliness.

In addition, most men are satiated and exhausted after the act as if they finished a grand buffet. If the act is going to drain your ambition and leave you pacified, it better be after an authentic and genuine victory. The amount of biological energy it must take to produce the literal essence of life must be immense. So when that is retained and reabsorbed into our being, we tap into our deepest and most powerful driving force. We can channel that into becoming fucking magnificent, so then we achieve and share magnificent experiences.

I needed to create a story that established my essence as a sacred substance. You don't trade gold for gummy bears, right? The greater value I give myself, my existence and potential, the more likely I actualize that belief. I intentionally amplified my distaste towards the act I obviously enjoyed indulging in so I could redirect my entire being into a higher harmony.

The part of you that you despise, other parts of you *love* it. Otherwise, you wouldn't be so torn to leave it behind, right? It must have a hidden value for you to reconcile that you are living but not yet able to articulate. Becoming aware of our patterns of blissful ignorance but still trying to outwit the consequences is a sinister game. The anticipation and build-up to doing what you know is not good for you becomes a dirty secret. You then deepen the intensity of your relationship with it.

Anticipation is like preparing for a heist. You have all these nerves and are planning to do something with obvious risk with no promised outcome, but we've convinced ourselves it will pay off, and we can outrun the consequences. It is not only the substance now but the build-up as you romanticize the arriving event. It's a boredom killer. It falsifies itself as a hope worth aspiring to when nothing else feels more rewarding.

If eating nothing is the only alternative to eating something delicious and harmful, you can't blame anybody for not choosing blatant starvation. The habits we choose have some form of sustaining us. So, we must entirely reconstruct a framework of sustainable highs.

I read books and books on compassion, grace, grit, overcoming, addiction, leadership, spirituality, and so much more.

I relapsed anyway.

I put in a ridiculous number of hours into 'bettering myself' and captivated all these mentalities that equipped me to walk somebody else out of their misery. All the while, I kept one toe in my own weak ways behind the scenes. If I could help another, I figured I was 'healed' enough to continue dabbling in my own bullshit.

Despite this one critical defect, I made leaps and bounds in my growth, serenity, self-respect, and confidence along the way. This taught me that the effort between all the relapses, the holistic expansion, and the praying was still amounting to a heck of a lot.

A dysfunction like addiction is not a diagnosis; it's a healing crisis. It's a story! An unfolding with a beginning, middle and end. We are stuck in the middle with an ignorance of direction and options. Just because we are unaware of our options and potential does not mean it does not exist.

A fine line with this is that we can do more harm if we start virtue-signalling ourselves as greater than others for our victory over ourselves. Our power is not in the boasting of that success but the celebrating of humility to level with others that there is no low too low to be loved, worth loving, and capable of redemption. If I can celebrate the humility of how pathetic and small my steps had to be to start stacking sustainable wins, then I can give hope to anybody willing to start just as small.

Nemesis

Nemesis is the Greek goddess of divine retribution and balance. She represents justice, especially in punishing excessive pride or arrogance and ensuring that no one becomes too powerful or fortunate without consequence. Nemesis restores equilibrium by bringing down those disrespecting the natural order of the gods.

In myths, she is often depicted as a figure who delivers punishment to mortals or gods who act arrogantly or unjustly. For example, she is associated with the story of Narcissus, the beautiful but vain youth who fell in love with his reflection. Nemesis punished him for arrogance by luring him to a pool, where he became so obsessed with his image that he wasted away.

In short, Nemesis symbolizes fairness, revenge, and the inevitable consequences of one's actions. That's why Nemesis has been used as a term for the ultimate adversary. The challenge of a proper Nemesis will prod at your weakness to taunt your absolute potential. It may be perceived as a challenge or insult, but the spirit of Nemesis is to conspire for your finest to come forth.

Perhaps a quality of mine that doubles as both a virtue and a vice is how obsessively I play my own Devil's advocate. Has it become evident in this book now that I'm quite comfortable taunting myself? I think I've tried to twist the fabric of reality to my will to prove to myself that the consequences are real and consistent.

Quitting porn was difficult and shameful. So, rather than just overcoming it, I thought I could outsmart the consequences by becoming multi-dimensionally jacked to compensate. Perfectionism is unreasonable, right? Everybody else has self-soothing habits, and *they* get by just fine. Can't I keep one bad habit in moderation and still be an epic, positively influential person?

Possibly. But I'm not trying to get by 'just fine.' I'm trying to get through life with an infectious enthusiasm that stems from the appropriate (and natural) sort of deprivation that compels me to get out of my comfort and cowardice. I believe our magnificence is a natural state. So, eliminating unnatural pleasures and habits means returning to that magnificence.

But while bargaining with my self-respect to keep that habit, I made a guinea pig out of my own soul. I wanted to see how far I could twist reality (without harming anybody else—or so I thought) before it snapped back on me.

The results? I prolonged my own self-inflicted suffering because... (I stopped here for a very long time to find the most honest answer. I hate stating it) all this effort to become 'exceptional' made me think I could be the exception. If I was outstanding in all other facets of life, can't I keep one crutch to lean on in the absence of that holistic intimacy I yearn for?

But that 'crutch' insinuates I was wounded and needed something to lean on, doesn't it? I figured that when this ultimate opportunity of intimacy arrives, I could replace and channel all that energy to an epic woman and the life we co-create. But the woman of such magnitude would reasonably hope that I conquered these internal wars before I found her. She would deserve the peace of mind of the pure self-control I preached about.

I told myself, 'I don't bargain with cowards.' But then I also had to identify an internal voice as a coward. There was *some* victory overpowering what I concluded as a proclaimed 'pathetic cry' for self-soothing, but the voice of unmet needs is persistent. This is a major point of shifting from trying to 'manage' the monster to 'befriending' the monster.

I still identified the 'coward' as a monster. But I was tiptoeing to a more and more vivid conclusion that the 'monster' is my fear of loneliness. I, a man with a basic and deep yearning for meaningful connection and intimacy, now called myself cowardly for craving love.

I had to apologize to myself for many self-hating years for belittling what I now know to be my purest driving force. This appropriated desire is a fucking gift. It is a force that compels all that I am to my finest. To fabricate a peak experience of sensual connection and normalize it into selfish escape is an absolute failure of what I consider my ultimate design. I was literally surrendering my miracle-creating essence to something that couldn't care less for me.

How could I be surprised that I lacked energy and ambition when I was corrupting my system of desire? I was fabricating success through what I consider the ultimate primal drive of creation. I was dumb enough to think I could outsmart the most divine aspect of our biology.

I cannot wage war on myself. I cannot overpower, run from, or destroy a part of myself in a productive fashion. I must console and inspire my wounded and fearful parts to a harmonious end.

So, what did I conclude as better than fabricated sex? It had to be larger than life. Sex in its ultimate form is love fully actualized to perpetuate life itself. In the wise words of Loonie-Tunes characters who've been blown up and beaten repeatedly, 'If you can't beat 'em, join em!'

There is no 'beating' (in my estimation) one of the best experiences life has to offer. There is only building a life in complement to things *that* amazing. So, I turned my entire life into a playground of redefining and maximizing love on a personal, relational, and spiritual level. I want to play the same game that sex does at its finest. I want to live in such a way that I give myself the same absolute focus, effort and enthusiasm that I would give to earning an orgasm.

How can I act as a man in this one life to amplify creation, love, courage and freedom in every word and action? I can filter all my life through this question. Every experience becomes a way of play to actualize my ultimate becoming and who I am meant to grow alongside. And if you've ever had a fulfilling orgasm, you know how it leaves you in a giddy, exhausted satisfaction.

A purposeful life thoroughly lived does the exact same thing.

In the endless options before me, I can always ask myself, 'What do I win by doing this?' I have to conclude that anything that costs or threatens my self-respect is a stupid game. I am in constant pursuit of what I now optimally explain as an orgasmic lifestyle.

Sometimes, the whimpering voice of unmet needs can still barge in during solitude. And I still enjoy a lot of solitude. But I've concerned myself with being too busy *living*! My relentless curiosity returned the best of that wounded inner child and gave him his favourite part of living back. A courageous pursuit of wonder.

Now, everything I've never tried *is* the journey. I seek the anticipation that I can make this new day like no other. The alternative belief is to anticipate how I will cap off another day mundanely lived to soothe my own fear and faithlessness that love is limited or out of reach. My whole world slowly transformed from a lonely audience to a joyful participant.

The anger that inspired my own personal justice was calm. This anger was calculated. This is the anger that spiritually hugs my wounded inner child who knew no better. This is not the belittling but the befriending of the self-proclaimed demon. It's like being mad at your kid for having no options for play and doing something chaotic out of frustration. Instead, you apologize by taking them on an adventure that's so captivating that they forget they were ever frustrated or lonely.

The gnawing temptation dwindled as I found new definitions of richness. I quit trying to outsmart my desire and wanted to forge the new truth in my brain that allowed me not to flinch when I looked at my own soul. If I had a chink in my armour, it was of my own making.

There is no shame in wanting a damn kiss on the forehead and a multiple-minute hug when life rains down with its unfathomable fuckery. There is no shame in desiring deep and profound support. There is no shame in craving to be desired. There is no misdeed in fumbling forward into love. We are all on our first trip through life. The difficulty is the spice of a worthwhile struggle.

The battles were many. But now I realize what they mean when they say you can lose many battles and win the war. We are made new every day and every moment. You're *that* capable.

This is again where we define fear as self-preserving and love as others-amplifying. It's also the most humanizing, humbling experience of my life. So, if you want to ask where people really find proof of God, I'd have to say it is in our deepest suffering. If you can't find God, you're not looking low enough. It is in the transforming of pain, tragedy, fear and anger into something profoundly beautiful.

My friend Marcus told me that in his indigenous heritage, they say, 'Those more deeply in pain are closer to the Gods.' To me, this meant that when we are suffering, all cluttered thoughts fall away, and we cling closer to the absolute essentials to survive that pain. As the cancer community says, 'A healthy man has a thousand wishes; a sick man has but one.'

We continue validating every reason to stay down and identify as a failed, miserable waste of a person. But it's like body-swapping into your best friend for a day: What would it look like to treat yourself as somebody unflinchingly worth fighting for one moment and day at a time? Could you slowly design a new life and character despite a very real sense of self-hatred on their behalf? That is divine.

Be mad enough to make a difference because tolerance is how we got here, isn't it?

That's why it is said, 'Faith without work is dead.' It is not passive wishing and hoping. It is a labour of *love*. This is the act of pulling from a vision of a world not yet seen and slowly making it a reality. *That* is the twisting of reality that my wounded self was begging for. The dissatisfaction I sat on of this chapter for two years was the intuitive evidence I had not properly done myself justice *yet*!

Everybody bargains with their self-respect in different ways. To me, the bargaining came down to this fundamental battle with the grand vision of my life: Do I believe I can honestly reach my highest potential while consistently engaging in the acts that make me despise myself? Can I live the rest of my life acting with the audacity that the best is on its way to me while sustaining a fear of being found out at any moment that I am not genuine? Do I believe I can fabricate my convictions and think I did my best for those I love?

It seems clear that there is a dramatic difference in outcome between truly walking my talk and attempting to fabricate my worthiness. This is why I was able to mention that fake Big Gift Energy is like being a coward in a conqueror's clothing. Even if I somehow arrived to fully manifest the life of my greatest dreams, the absolute greatest terror would manifest as foreboding joy.

Foreboding Joy 2.0

There is that crazy question of 'Why are we afraid of good things?' But the real question is, 'Why are we committed to believing we do not deserve good things?' I'm doubling down on Foreboding joy as one of the most gut-wrenching, sinister fears that could subtly manifest. This terror is nurtured in the festering of doubt and discontent. So, we must fight it with valiant audacity in our expression for that and those we love.

Foreboding Joy is the idea that joy is interrupted by the thoughts of 'What if something bad happens?' But when nothing else is wrong, our fears of unworthiness manifest themselves as 'the bad thing that could happen.'

All of life's desires could fall upon us, but if our fears of unworthiness silence us from wholeheartedly believing we are worth the good fight to sustain it, the fear is manifested by default. Our humility to be seen as we are, for *all* that we are, is directly proportional to the depth and quality of relationships and experiences we will sustain in this life.

There is no moment like the present to declare our value worth fighting for. We can lie and lie and try to keep our bullshit flying high - we see proof of it everywhere in the relationships, celebrities and idols we worship. All until those people are found out and forced to rebuild from a foundation of humility.

A mansion built on lies is not worth keeping. Your spirit can be dying inside while your surface-level razzle-dazzle convinces the world otherwise. The truth always wins, so wouldn't we rather be on its side?

It all came down to this: Do I really believe I could ever feel love if I never gave the *whole* me? Do I *want* to subscribe to the idea that some secrets and sides of me are unforgivable? That would have me surrender my opportunity to feel truly accepted before I ever give somebody the chance.

Doesn't it make more sense to humble myself and be seen as I am for *all* I am? I want to know I fumbled forward valiantly with my self-respect purified. I want to reciprocate that full surrender and say it genuinely when we tell each other we are worth it. I don't want the best connections in life to be haunted by my own ghost. I want an embrace to be exactly that and not just a successful sales pitch of who I hope they see me to be.

I genuinely looked up and out the window at the pure darkness of a 2:00 AM night, and the Nemesis voice asked again, "You think you're strong enough?"

I hesitated.

My track record would justify my hesitation. But my track record is a memory, not a prophecy. It's a warning sign that I am always one step away from being stupid. But that makes me respect myself as a worthy adversary. I contend with a future that I believe to be profound and meaningful. One that is simple and universal. One that allows me room to consider no failure to be final unless I quit. Miracles and goodness aren't dead just because sometimes I feel lonely and afraid. We are made of endless redemption.

That is how human I am. And that is why I see myself in every wounded man or woman who bargains with their own worth. May I walk forward as though being human - flaws and all - is enough. It *has* to be. Because it's all we are.

Perhaps one day, you'll be pissed off enough to reach out and say you can't do it alone. Because love uses imperfect people like you and me, to heal imperfect people like you and me.

Chapter 18

A Deranged Future

All of art, entertainment, and every product is a dare to make you feel a certain way. The creator's dare is that reality is richer for using or affiliated with their product or experience. A horror film is a dare in which a creator can portray a story so ominous and tempting that you'll agree - even *pay* - to see if your senses can be convinced into a fabricated terror. For fun, of course! To watch somebody's house come alive as ghosts slam doors or a serial killer stalks an unexpected innocent. A tame way to unwind after a long day's work, right?

The same goes for every love story. You fall in love with flawed characters and follow an unfolding of highs and lows with them. They aren't even real people, yet you take the chance to see it through in the hope that love prevails. We want to believe that the fight is worthwhile and the sacrifices we throw at the universe can kick back in ways that make it *all* worthwhile. Not all love stories are made equal, yet we take the dare to be compelled in such an emotional way to pass the time.

It's the same with every comedy. You can follow some strange characters through their tale of mishaps and find a way to chuckle through misfortune. It simulates how we find lightheartedness in everything and are morally shocked at the humour made of dark situations. Yet, it tickles our fancy anyway. Not every flavour of humour lands the same for everybody, but we take the dare.

Consider the profound effect that just observing these stories has on us. I'll reference back to my kid brother thinking he could be Batman himself after just one movie. We judge whether we are bigger or smarter than the ghosts and monsters of horror movies. We judge whether we are courageous enough to live a life of romance. We absorb the spirit of humour and wit to be the jester in tough times, making us the most ideal friends to have. All of this is fine and fair play, best experienced in moderation.

I realized my own tolerance to personal growth, spiritual, and mindset material has also grown. I'll happily take one profound quote or concept from an entire book now, as I've seen many book and educational concepts overlap.

I've begun looking for more provocative topics like understanding childhood PTSD and the exploration of how 'evil' unknowingly manifests in everyday people. It is still mental, emotional and spiritual 'play' for me, but the content intensity has dramatically increased. I know because the things I'm learning and fascinated about are increasingly unpalatable for average conversation. If I'm to understand and wage war on worldly sorrow, I willingly build my tolerance to the true tragedies of the human experience. I do not want to flinch when love needs to transcend fear and misunderstanding of another's pain and actions.

You can be desensitized to *anything* with great enough exposure to it. Talented musicians don't know how wonderful their music is because they've practiced each song a hundred times. Yet it is a goosebumps-level novelty to the new listener. Horror movies become predictable, and the gore is underwhelming once you've witnessed enough. The romantic cliches no longer have any flair, and the shock value of jokes isn't as spicy in overwhelming doses. The product, art, or entertainment must increase provocativeness to capture our attention. So, we have created more and more aggressive, taboo, and devastating content to make our dare as creators and entertainers deliver as promised.

Your attention is our business. Literally.

Entertained Into Oblivion

I'm trying to keep this book spicy with my version of provocative content to keep you turning pages. I want to help you arrive at a state of grace, confidence, and a spirit of excitement for the future by the end of this. I risk losing your interest just by explaining that. It's like explaining a joke; you're either in tune and get it, or its punchline falls short if it must be explained. Any product or experience demands that the value and message speak for itself. You don't want to be told to be brave, you want opportunities worth being brave for. In a world painting itself as a dystopia beyond repair, we are convinced it's reasonable to sit back and pleasure ourselves as the world burns.

In the spirit of that, I feel compelled to talk about our tolerance levels in accordance with the dares we are soon to be receiving. We are so barraged with content that our threshold for intensity and stimulation is wildly different than somebody outside a lifestyle with the internet. This is a deranged future because our nervous system and minds are genuinely processing information and stimulation far beyond the range of all history's normalcy.

Products and drugs are getting smarter. False reality is competing to be better than the real world. *That* is a dare not to take lightly. And you best believe it wouldn't be an impending dare if somebody weren't radically confident in their product to convince you of that. Some may consider the following deranged. Others may be overjoyed by the prospects.

Enter super-stimulus. Super-stimulus parades itself as normal but is slightly exaggerated from what nature provides. It highjacks our attention and desire through flavour, chemicals, visuals, and whatever other compelling form. A positive form of super-stimulus would be making captivating educational content. But the negative side is that it can cause addiction, over-consumption, and compulsive habits.

It affects animals in nature just as well. Female frogs prefer males with louder, deeper, or more frequent croaks. An artificial playback of amplified croaks often attracts females more than real frogs. That one false performance hijacked their entire reproductive drive. Now imagine how the industries have twisted everything at their disposal to vie for our attention and desires and capitalize on our insecurities.

The ultimate issue here is how super-stimuli in entertainment, processed foods, porn, fashion, design, and media are all more easily accessible than natural satisfactions. It is now a genuine effort against the modern grain to revert your primal survival senses back to health and moderation. Most of us are so normalized to hyper-stimulation that our bodies and minds would be confused and disorientated by healthier and natural alternative lifestyles. We would have to detox and endure the withdrawal effects to see what power it has subtly entrenched in us.

But the industries do not concern themselves with your inability to control yourself. They will still take their bets on society to make a buck. Some of these bets sound like:

"I bet I can create an artificially intelligence girlfriend/boyfriend better than a real person. Where you can alter their appearance and cater to all your curious desires better and less shamefully than dealing with a real person." Even *trying* this will permanently corrupt your sense of possibility and bargain with an easier alternative than trying to manage a real-life relationship. This is porn on steroids.

There are real people who've already married their holographic partners and sex dolls. You'd have to so radically abandon the possibility of a meaningful human relationship to bother legally marrying an *idea*. Yet this is an impending future around the corner that will only grow more alluring by the day. Somebody's business model is waging war on human connection.

Another sinister dare of propaganda that is already in motion sounds like, "I bet we can normalize alcohol or party drugs so casually as a society that we can convince everybody who *isn't* partying to be the boring ones. Playing on the edge of oblivion as a pastime is perfectly acceptable. The people who try to ask you to take a break and practice sobriety just aren't as fun as you."

Even trying this permanently opens the reality that you can fabricate your courage, adventurousness, and ability to flirt and relax. This is a slippery slope of societal normality that we incorporate into daily life because just being ourselves isn't relaxing enough. That discontent is your internal warning system that you're falling away from a satisfying life. Mind-altering substances turn off the warning system well and convincingly enough that you think you can continue to avoid it. Meanwhile, the discontent and lack of courage to adventure and face your anxiousness grows more intimidating by the day.

We will soon wage war on authenticity when a dare says, "I bet this artificial intelligence can take enough samples of your voice that you can build deep-fake personalized videos for clients. They will be none-the-wiser that it isn't personal at all. Your creativity and reputation will be entirely outsourced. You can basically print money on our behalf if you sell us your personality. It will only cost your conscience… if you ever had one."

This saves influencers incredible amounts of time yet dances on the edge of insincerity and creates a false connection. It will also make anybody with any remote amount of media presence an identity to be stolen with minimal effort. We will be waging war on reality itself through and alongside AI.

As for another dare, "I bet this video game's culture and economy can be so deeply entertaining that it's more satisfying to develop respect and prestige here than in real life." When life gets so stressful, any easier alternative to feeling valued and connected to others will lean heavily on virtual communities and cultures.

You don't have to overcome flaws and insecurities when you can align an identity with a virtual character of your ever-changeable design. Changing the well-being of our real body and mind is far more expensive, timely, and difficult. But buying 'skins' of cool clothes, weapons, and customizable ways to express yourself will be a hundred times cheaper in effort, time, and money than in real life. Instead of having real-world features in your home, you could just have a place to eat, poop, and sleep while every resource in the real world is funnelled to the virtual world of your preference. Your body and mind will just become a driver for the character you genuinely prefer to live in a world of your choosing. This can easily outweigh the value you put on this body and the situation the real world has offered you.

Play Wisely

The thing is that these above-stated dares are already well and thriving in our world. Sobriety, community, intimacy, and even reality are being contended with. The razzle-dazzle and all varieties of highs have become so compelling and convincing that you must have quite a backbone to refrain from such things now.

I would not dare ask anybody to deny certain pleasures and entertainment because some might take it too far. I think it's a beautiful testament to our creativity and strangeness in all the ways we've found to enjoy this life. Even though there are some very acceptable blanket statements like, 'DON'T TRY HEROIN!' But these are more subtle temptations available to us all.

In fact, I would incline people to dip their toes in things they trust themselves to manage. This plethora of pleasures is bizarre proof that we have been so safe for so long that the toys get cooler and the pleasures get more flavourful by the day. Perhaps there is virtue in refraining entirely, but I could not offer that perspective as I'd be a hypocrite. But because I've experienced different temptations and gone too far, I've grown a character and conviction of deeper satisfaction with the raw world and humanity before us.

I'd be lying if I said I never got a revelation that altered my reality from a high I initially swore I'd never partake. I was just appreciative that I waited long enough to have a very conscious relationship with myself and substances before I tried it. I would never deny anybody else the freedom and novelty to find out for themselves.

This world is truly our playground. But our self-trust may be in direct proportion to the depth of our dopamine addictions. Growing bored and unappreciative of a pleasure is a blessing in two ways. One way is that our spirit demands novelty and is beckoning us to break the cycle. The other is that it creates a space to revive our curiosity about all the other options before us. That displeasure and abused tolerance may beckon the moment we reorganize and revive the variety of raw pleasures available to us.

If you want to challenge your tolerances and which substances may hold power over you, dedicate 2-4 weeks to cutting them out individually. Cold stop. Not weaning off. Feel the full disruption of the discomfort mentally, emotionally and physically to prove to yourself that you have control over your habits and substances.

Please take note of your irritability and consider what alternatives you try to replace it with. It can be a sinister game to hop from one dependent substance to the next. You are as powerful as you are independent from substances to regulate yourself. When your self-regulation is as frail as missing your morning coffee or your phone dying, you realize how deep the modern dependence runs.

A Deranged Future

It's a strange affliction to be at war with all the pleasures available to us now. Perhaps our future generation may laugh at us, just as we have laughed at the generation we didn't understand before us.

We are all a bit strange, and we grow stranger by the day as we deepen our practice of the oddities and pleasures of life. We came here to play as much as we came to build the future. If we built a future and never enjoyed the journey, we could never expect those after us to find our ways compelling. Yes, meaningful sacrifices must be made, and we will all face those independently.

If you're going to play, play with your entire being. Just as we shouldn't half-ass a meaningful aspiration, we should also be all-out and captivated in our play. You can't half sleep; you must actually be unconscious. So, you can't commit fully to your joy either if you will guilt yourself for it later.

Save yourself the guilt and remind yourself that you were brought into this world through orgasmic pleasure. Play and pleasure are the source of our being. If you want to bring your ultimate self into the future, you cannot resent the effort that got you there. Play is sustenance for the soul. Just ensure that while you harvest joy, your life force and values are not also harvested in the process.

CHAPTER 19

Stigma

After doing a speaking engagement at a university on the topic of imposter syndrome, a student asked me, "I'm afraid of the stigma associated with using some of the free mental health resources at the school. How do I overcome this block?"

Stigma is defined as a disgrace associated with a particular circumstance, quality, or person. I had three points from that one question:

1. If you're afraid of the stigma, the stigma has already won over you. *You* validate the stigma over yourself by letting the fear of its possibility hover over you. People do not fear what they are confident doesn't apply to them.

2. Having resources that you're afraid to use is the same as saying you're hungry but are too good for a handout. It's not like anybody is physically blocking you from acquiring your nourishment. You're starving yourself over the mere *idea* that somebody will look down on you for accepting help outside your understanding. This leads to point three.

3. When I ask *who* will belittle you, few people can actually offer names. Regardless, anybody who belittles your growth or well-being is not your friend. You don't stop taking care of yourself because some jerk points out an imperfection. You have a duty to your own well-being to try any and all resources to not only just get by but experience the full range of your health.

The most confident and well-rounded people I know have near-constant mentors, coaches, support groups, rituals, and practices to keep themselves maintained. Even then, they catch themselves coming up short in their balance. So, if you are afraid to even start using mental health, spiritual, emotional, or physical rehab resources, it's absolutely expected that you experience frequent turbulence in your peace and well-being.

Nobody is an island. Nobody is self-made. Nobody gets a user manual for the human experience when you come out of the womb. Even the greatest strategists, scientists, athletes, performers and leaders have blind spots and are accident-prone. The finest we have to offer ourselves is still, at its core, just another human doing their best.

If you fear being aligned to a stigma, then the default outcome is that you *keep* the problem. Conversely, when you've conquered a previous state of being that you feel disgraced about, it becomes a war cry for others that recovery is possible.

This chapter is dedicated to a few friends who now carry their stigmas as badges of honour. They are living survival guides for others. Would you be opposed to taking advice on serenity from a person who overcame psychosis and psychotic breaks? Would you refuse advice about balance from somebody who's conquered Borderline Personality Disorder? Would you take sobriety advice from an ex-drug dealer and addict? Or do you want all of your advice from somebody who never really suffered like you have?

The people who've lived through the turmoil have the most to offer you. Not to belittle education, but real-life trumps what a textbook can never offer in human connection. A textbook can't say, "I'm here for you" Or "Me too."

My stress of this chapter is to suggest that every and all modalities of recovery, therapy, transformation and adventure is a higher response to our insecurities and worries than hiding. No attempt to better ourselves should be shamed or considered taboo. We should rather support and promote curiosity about different modalities of thought and healing so we have more to offer one another. Everybody's journey, trauma and path to serenity is unique. Nobody can do that work for you.

So, if somebody is in the way of your pursuit of self-discovery and healing, they might just be terrified of their own soul. You're healing might expose that they have their own to do too. Or that they were even part of the issue.

Anybody wanting to see the best of you wouldn't advocate for ignorance. Real friends are not afraid of your evolution. True friends do not flinch at the murkiness of mankind because we are all always one step away from misfortune.

I will share three deep transformation stories of dear friends who have master-crafted their sorrows into survival guides. Their realities are taboo to the average person and are experiences many people would rather not associate with or care to notice. It's easier to pretend the hardships and terrors of the world are not happening all around you, but the difficulties of everyday people around you are alive and well. All we have is one another. Let me prove that.

Marcus - From Dealing Drugs to Dealing Recovery

I graduated alongside my fairly small-town drug dealer, Marcus. We were on fond terms back in the day, to the point he BBQ-ed me taquitos at a hundred-person bush party in high school. We rarely affiliated otherwise. His nickname was tattooed on his neck by the age of 16 and was slanging gold and silver chains. The chains were more than style but also an expression of power, lest somebody act up and weapons need to be drawn.

He fits most, if not all, of the stereotypes that scream 'gang member.' He has the stories, the money and the gold grills at a young age to prove it. But he was a man of many faces and interests. He could throw on a suit and talk business with entrepreneurial buddies or be a barefoot hippie with other friends. He was a product of many associations but had little to no consistent individuality.

Fast-forward his life a few years into young adulthood, where the lifestyle of chasing a high left a line of devastated relationships and close friends overdosing. Marcus admits he was everything you'd *never* want in a romantic partner. He cheated on every girlfriend he ever had and had no remorse. All until his own failed suicide attempt landed him in the hospital.

He woke up to the person he expected least to be by his side. It was his recent ex who was aware of his cheating and wrongdoing, yet she did not flinch to support his recovery. Marcus's failed attempt at overdosing on pills lead to therapy to learn even to speak again. He experienced radio silence from so-called friends and realized his only connection to many was the drugs he provided. Now, his lifeline was somebody who had every reason to have no sympathy, yet she stayed and supported him anyway.

Marcus admitted himself to rehab, where he met his newfound friend and now co-sponsor to addicts, Sheldon. Marcus and Sheldon have stayed sober since and have committed that gratitude of recovery support to now sponsoring addicts in return. Marcus's previous lifestyle of darkness, deception and selfishness allowed him a powerful space to sit confidently among society's most hardened and downtrodden. Marcus and Sheldon have since held space for over 200 individual men as they reconcile their habits into a renewed life of sobriety.

I, myself, have leaned on Marcus a handful of times and find myself profoundly lucky to share space with him. We were not close in our previous lives, but in this new shared trajectory of waging war on suicide rates and amplifying healthy relationships, we have become inseparable friends. I now have the pleasure of witnessing him navigate fatherhood and celebrate the *failure* of his suicide attempt. Desperation is a hell of a motivator. But nobody is beyond recovery and rehabilitation. The opposite of addiction is connection.

Marcus may have previously been a supplier in the world of addictions, but now he has one of the most expansive testimonies of recovery I've ever witnessed. I attribute much of my serenity to some of the lessons he has shared with me. He has also challenged me to be a man of integrity. Thank you for sharpening my character, Marcus. You've been instrumental to my growth. It's a pleasure to brag about the man you've become and are still becoming.

Rachel - Homeless to Heroism

Buckle up for this one; Rachel's story is riddled with every flavour of the trauma rainbow. Being diagnosed with Borderline Personality Disorder, her foundation is torn between warring realities from the beginning. Having been in therapy from the age of 12, the stigma of 'broken,' 'untrustworthy,' 'inconsistent,' 'crazy,' and so much more could never let her own head feel like home.

Her young adulthood was riddled with stays between different trap houses, bouts of homelessness, a cocaine addiction, physically and mentally abusive relationships, and two separate admittances to mental hospitals.

She remembers sitting patiently awaiting a room in the mental hospital as the nurses frantically tried to calm other screaming patients. A nurse offered Rachel earplugs, and she softly denied them with a hand extended, saying, "No, thank you. I really relate to these people."

She fondly recollects John, a patient who would scream and smash his head into the wall until he was given his red crayon. He then shifted to the most joyous singing as he scribbled his red drawings.

All the while since her early 20's, she has been catering to a musical career that would not be diminished in any circumstance. She wrote songs while homeless in the backseat of her car for two months, would busk on the side of the streets for breakfast money, and now uses it as a platform to advocate for mental health and survivors of sexual assault. She taught me that trauma needs to live somewhere outside our body. That's why we have art.

After more than forty unhelpful therapists over two decades, she finally met one focused on results rather than prolonging the hourly sessions to get paid.

Rachel said, "I'm only giving you ten sessions to work your magic."

The therapist responded, "I'll do it in five."

Rachel's tree was thoroughly shaken within three. She received no-bullshit advice that finally simplified Rachel's warring realities and the choices she had before her. Sometime later, as Rachel grew an excitement and appreciation for her therapy sessions, she eventually was told, "You no longer meet the criteria for borderline personality disorder."

It may have taken fifteen years, but Rachel had arrived at a state of control over impulsive behaviours, suicidal ideation and emotional instability. May I stress 'control over,' not 'freedom from,' impulsive behaviours as the human experience has no cheat code for the troubles we all ruminate on. To merely have the tools to regain her ownership and control of her story is a war cry she now shares throughout her musical career.

Alongside that, she has had cleaning businesses that did and could have kept her wallet full, yet she was called to work with the local youth homeless shelters instead. Making barely above minimum wage, she finds much greater fulfillment in equipping teens with similar tools she was given to overcome their addictions and traumas.

These kids are those who've been entirely abandoned, abused and left to desperation with no life skills.

People like Rachel offer these youth the first time they are treated with respect and validated in their sorrows and anger towards the world. These kids call her 'Mama Rachel' and have kept personalized inspirational notes Rachel has left them. In bouts of being back on the streets for months at a time, these kids would have lost everything again, but they would hold on to their letters from Rachel.

On top of that, Rachel has interrupted and stopped many counts of pedophilia when late 20-year-old men prey upon these under-aged homeless girls. Rachel has helped these young girls realize the manipulation they've been under and cut these tragic men from their lives. She equates the sensation of empowering these young girls and exposing pedophiles to how people celebrate a touchdown at the Superbowl. Taking down predators and helping troubled kids live better lives is Rachel's sport, and she is an unsung all-star.

I'm glad I've enriched some of the clarity in your everyday struggles, Rachel Geek. But it is my great privilege to flex on you as a friend, artist, and role model. I admire you to the ends of the earth. The world is richer to have you here.

Lucas - A Grudge with the Devil

I met Lucas through the 'gratitude' hashtag while networking for *An Arsenal of Gratitude*. He was one of few people whose content struck me so profoundly about his journey to discover himself. Little did I know he was battling with bouts of psychosis. He explained it as a spiritual allergy to alcohol and marijuana. In one of his worst episodes, he was celebrating marijuana being newly legal in Canada and found himself unknowingly arguing with homeless people at 3:00 AM.

Lucas (In his words) recounts: *The part of my last two episodes where I was lost in downtown Red Deer, was when my phone had died on my way to pick a bone with Satan. I felt I was doing Jesus a favour and providing some support for him when he returned, which I thought was that night. I was God's right-hand man on my way to do the devil dirty; don't ask me how.*

I was hearing voices, off my meds and wearing a hi-vis hoodie. I was walking around aimlessly and cold with my hands over my heart, yelling, "Jesus Christ, Jesus Christ, Jesus Christ." It was a chant to fend off voices while listening to Tupac.

Though Lucas did not explicitly struggle with substance addiction, his favourite scripture that kept him sober during his worst psychotic break was this: *"Be alert and of sober mind. Your enemy, the devil, prowls around like a roaring lion looking for someone to devour."*[vi] - 1 Peter 5:8 NIV

Lucas read countless books on finances, spirituality, personal development and philosophy to root himself in a reality in which he could be powerful. Despite his best efforts for a time, he was swinging back and forth between an attempt to act as a leader with his teachings on social media and feeling a complete lack of grounding. His attempt to verbalize his growth and convictions were as pure as they come, yet he was still amid self-discovery. His swings of confidence and utter lack of control were necessary as he navigated the murk of his troubled soul.

As far as my conversations with him, all his efforts were genuine and instrumental to the peace he had yet to find. I received a late call from him during a midnight winter and remembered the timidity in his voice as he expressed his fear in the mental black hole he walked himself into. He was practicing shadow work, studying your own dark side to understand, respect, and love all the dimensions of your human experience. As somebody who has done this and gone too far himself, in some attempts to go into your own spirit alone, you can be convinced that you are entirely a corrupt, terrible, sick creation.

I was grateful that I could suddenly throw him an emotional and spiritual lifeline through a story of my own shadow work. I had to admit my capacity to do things against my own best judgment, be selfish, manipulative, cruel, and so much more. Despite these qualities, my commitments to a life of integrity, paying it forward, and the high road gained depth since I've felt what it's like to profit cheaply and at the expense of others.

Shadow work is (among many things) an intentional effort to listen and study your own sick thoughts to practice discarding them and pave your own reality worth living and loving. That night, over a call with Lucas, I shared things I hoped would never have to surface. But in that moment, it became a humanizing state of connection that shed his fear and shame over his self-discovery.

He later sought guidance regarding spiritual warfare at the same church where he had one of his darkest moments. In the thick of his last psychotic break, he tried to cut his neck on a handicap sign in a frantic attempt to comprehend the delusion of the abandonment of Jesus's second coming. He thought Jesus came and left without him.

Lucas states thereafter: *I agreed to go for counselling with the pastor of that church, which was part of the spiritual deliverance. I can remember it quite well. I agreed to get delivered from demonic oppression, although I wasn't expecting what the pastor was about to work through me. I actually got delivered from Lust, Loneliness, Disobedience, and Fear, which were four spirits. This later became an epic testimony I gave in front of eighty people.*

After we made sure I was saved and my name was written in the Book of Life, a following counselling session unfolded. The pastor said, "OK, so I'm going to be looking at you, but I'm going to talk to the spirits inside you."

Fast-forward a bit, and he continued, "If there are any evil spirits inside of Lucas, come forward in the name of Jesus."

Sure as shit, I subconsciously tensed up and leaned forward.

"How long have you been with Lucas?" Asked the pastor.

Something involuntarily came from my mouth, "I Grew up with him."

After a long wrestle against spiritual forces, by the authority of Jesus, I took a deep breath of newfound peace. But not without being left completely exhausted.

Lucas explains psychosis as if being on an airplane; when you reach a certain altitude, you start to lose a sense of gravity. With no threshold to return to 'normalcy,' it's basically 'by the grace of God' that you come back to land safely. He was able to ween off of anti-depressants entirely with his newfound practices for peace and self-regulation.

Lucas quotes, "There is no threshold between the reality of normalcy and psychosis."

He now shares his testimony about navigating the many voices and thoughts that attempt to shake our serenity. He continues to send me messages celebrating his growth, excitement for life, and taking meaningful risks. He gets to take those seasons of mental, emotional, and spiritual terror and turn them into somebody else's peace of mind since so few are willing to share a topic made taboo by society.

I asked him what inspires his efforts to share his story and pay it forward despite other's inability to understand and relate. He said, "I have a grudge with the Devil. He tried to take my serenity. So now I want to show others that peace is real."

Seeing you grow and share your journey is an absolute pleasure, my friend.

Do you see the variety of people transforming their hardships into service to others? Ex-drug dealers become sponsors. The homeless can become mentors, and the psychotic can help others navigate serenity. Very little, if nothing, cannot be overcome and transformed into relatable servitude for others.

All We Have is Each Other

Leave love notes for your friends for no reason. It takes so little to speak life into another person and shift their trajectory to something meaningful. We hold on to those notes with white knuckles, harder than most anything else we own. I know personally, as well as any friend that I shared above when it's all about yourself, it sure feels easy to give up when you've decided you're worthless. But it is our gift to one another to never lose faith in one another as a redemption story in the making.

You cannot heal in the same environment that made you ill. This world offers countless free options to break free from our environment, routine and spiralling despair. There are churches, meditations, yoga, sober groups, animal shelter volunteering, adventure pages, book studies, community events, and so much more. There are enough lonely people craving the exact same bare necessity connections that could completely rejuvenate our well-being.

I've heard from more than ten other friends, only in our twenties, that if it wasn't for their cat or dog, they might not be here either. We were made for one another. Giving that cat or dog a good life trumped every selfish thought and gave them a lifeline reason to sustain themselves on that animal's behalf.

We are all survivors of bizarre, strange, and misunderstood lives. Yet today is not done with us. We have survived every one of our hardest days. As much as we doubt it, we are built for it. So much has happened to us against our will, yet our capacity to thrive despite it is the most rebellious act of love and faith for life that we can offer one another.

I cannot promise that you will never suffer, but I can promise that your courage to hold on to faith that the future has something more to offer is what we can all lean on. There may be a day you are called upon for your hope to be a lifeline. Even if it shakes when it comes out of your mouth, it can be enough to save a life.

I've been wrung out with despair and hopelessness, too. That's why this whole journey is one wild, courageous dare. Merely caring for ourselves and nurturing our enthusiasm for life could be the lifeline somebody leans on one day. Serving your greatest good serves all others at the same time.

CHAPTER 20

Savage Servitude

A lack of negative traits does not suggest the presence of positive ones. This chapter essentially outlines immature vs. mature masculinity. I want to make this distinction abundantly clear so women can understand and men can sort themselves accordingly. It is an offering in the culture that screams about 'toxic masculinity'. I am not discrediting any women with the valiant qualities I am to speak on but emphasizing the gaps of value and belonging that prevent men from actualizing themselves.

I have developed from a self-proclaimed 'Nice Guy' to what I now understand as a Good Man. So, before any readers get their feathers all ruffled by the stated insecurities, first read this as a confession of sorts. Then, allow it to be living proof that self-actualization and the gathering of meaningful responsibility is a genuine path to a better life experience.

Masculinity does not request us to be merely decent. It requests us to be epic.

Evolutionarily Sexy

There is a terminology of 'Nice Guys' with this identity of a morally decent person that is also the most freely discarded in the world of intimacy. Nice guys seem to be victims of circumstance when a girl enjoys their company, only to truly give their love and attention to the 'bad boys.' Nice Guys loudly despise and claim themselves superior to others while losing to them on a near-constant basis. Nice guys aren't necessarily secret bad people, but they are boring. I can explain this on an evolutionary level.

In the upbringing of our civilizations as hunters and gatherers, scarcity and danger held the most attention of everybody. Any laziness or lacklustre energy towards the necessities of life would make you obsolete. Everybody had an essential role and responsibility to complement each other. If you were not dangerous, you were not at the top of the pecking order (or hierarchy) of providers and defenders. This made you not worth paying attention to compared to those of substantial stature and responsibility.

Scarcity created a constant pursuit of survival needs as comfort and overabundance were only an experience for the highest of royalty. Nice guys were certainly not those in positions of royalty as ruthlessness would be essential to hold such a position. Nice Guys are never mistaken for anything close to royalty unless they hold up a front or create a facade of fake value. If you were 'too available,' then it meant you were not playing a substantial role in the community. The pilgrimage of maturity is the story of being cared for and becoming somebody who can care for others.

Responsibility is evolutionarily sexy.

If you're always available for a potential mate, you must also be overflowing with resources and dangerous enough to defend them. In addition, constant availability means that you are making your value convenient, which nothing worthwhile or significant ever came conveniently. Therefore, modern-day Nice Guys are treated as a convenience, not something to be pursued. They've already surrendered their value without making the person they're attempting to attract respect the exclusivity of what they offer. So, it comes full circle as high-value characters eventually create their own scarcity as their value demands that only qualified individuals have access to what they bring to the table. Being too available with low standards of entry makes you a human doormat.

Your resources will be quickly used up, and there will be no repercussions or consequences for those who took advantage of you. If you have no place of authority or prowess to create consequences for this injustice of how others treat you, it is human nature embedded in our survival to capitalize on easy prey. It's hard to call it selfish if the Nice Guy who willingly offers the opportunity to be taken advantage of mistakes your acceptance of the offer as winning your favour. Creating an easy space to survive does not translate to true human connection. You are merely a refuge for people to use as they pursue what they really want.

After survival and safety, love and belonging come into play. Now, your compatibility can come into actualization. It makes sense that it doesn't quite matter if you're compatible in regards to love if you're starving and in danger. We will do anything to survive as the pain of deprivation forces us to radical action. After love and belonging, we create ourselves within the community to add continued value and growth. Otherwise, we become leeches of a system and will be kicked out for not reciprocating any sense of value for the cost of our existence. That's just raw, primitive nature for you.

After all these states of being are in development, we enter the highest layer of existence, which is self-actualization. Self-actualization is the space to be holistically well enough to prioritize space for mankind's transcendence. It is time for creativity and ingenuity.

This is no shallow task. This means you must tap into spaces of your human potential that society has never yet witnessed. That means we pursue curiosity and the unknown to such a degree that we overflow in well-being so dramatically that the community as a whole evolves. We stumble upon ideas, create new tools, and design new systems in this time of abundance. This space justifies thousands of generations that did not give up against all odds so that future generations can see a world that could not be created in our ancestor's lifetime. The ultimate act of faith is to endure everything to create this space.

The next generations will pave the future that ours will never see. Digging a foundation to hell so we can build a tower to heaven may mean our life's purpose is as simple as paying it forward. My sons may finish the tower, but I would only prolong the inevitable process if I did not start it.

He who plants the trees so their children may have shade has begun to understand the meaning of life. - Unknown

Evolutionarily Boring

Do you know who can't provide this space of self-actualization? People who are emotional doormats who can barely provide for or defend themselves. *Nice Guys*, if you will. Nice guys will delight in playing the hero, but only for as long as they are validated and placed on a podium for their actions. They wish to remain in this place and keep those they 'save' in their codependency to ensure their value. When their partner or reliant becomes self-sufficient and the Nice Guy's 'heroics' become obsolete, the Nice Guy becomes dramatically insecure. He has not yet become somebody of value or interest beyond surviving.

Nice Guys innately know that they lack well-rounded stability. They tend to place themselves in complementary situations and call it compatibility. Yet when their person or people rightfully empower themselves to be more independent, the Nice Guy invalidates them instead of celebrating their success. The Nice Guy grows insecure when those around them grow because of their fear of competition and lack of dedication to bettering themselves. They may have a crooked desire to keep their partner below or be afraid of the challenges of self-actualization, so they cannot rightly expect them to join them on that journey. It's a long-winded and twisted way of them justifying their value, yet not actually rising to the maximal occasion of their own life.

Nice Guys lack a sense of their uniqueness. They live in the dog-eat-dog world. Nice Guys are insecure around others whom they would consider superior. They would be uncomfortable if their partners were to spend time with anybody in a position that the Nice Guy cannot fulfill themselves. Nice Guys fail to recognize their worth, sometimes outright deny it out of self-doubt and prefer instant gratification to grander goals. They will sacrifice their dreams for people and lose themselves by clinging to others as they have not yet found how to love themselves.

A Nice Guy's intentions may be pure, but they unravel in a way that lacks stable longevity. They hope to feel desired, important, and perhaps responsible for something worthwhile. But their lack of self-adequacy is their downfall. There are worlds where Nice Guys can hold a good space for a while but become adverse and reluctant to step up and change when their comfort or worth is threatened.

In this now dog-eat-dog society, the Nice Guys from hunter-and-gatherer lineages are becoming the hunted and gathered. You cannot acquire love and belonging in a world where your original role to provide is now the bare minimum. Your emotional intelligence and character must evolve so there is somebody of substance to actually love and belong with beyond just existing together.

Good Men

Good Men are savage servants. Good Men crave responsibility that matters and understand that being a provider can be a privilege. These kinds of men who work ungodly hours only need a photograph of their partner and kid in their hard hat to outwork exhaustion.

Good Men have great boundaries, which means they are in tune with their worth. Good boundaries suggest that they understand the balance of respecting themselves while keeping others at the proper distance to respect them as well. This insinuates that they have the backbone to have the conversations demanded to accomplish this. Not that they are immaculate about it—or anything for that matter—but they are consistent and emotionally steady.

Good Men are the ones who show up when hell breaks loose. Good Men delight in worthy battles. Good Men understand meaningful sacrifice and do not resent paying the price when they believe in what they are fighting for. Good Men are mentally flexible and patient in their difficulties and duties. Good Men do not live for themselves and never claim to be self-made. Good Men see all the moving parts that make the world possible. They know their small, diligent, consistent action is enough to make whatever dent is demanded of their calling.

Good Men know how to say 'no'. Good Men say uncomfortable things and move in truth because they defend their values. Good Men do not let other men believe their bullshit. Good Men have a healthy relationship with their shortcomings and don't flinch in making mistakes as they constantly live on the edge of their capabilities. Good Men tend to have a small circle as they understand the preciousness of time and the quality worth reciprocating.

Good Men make selfish and insincere people nervous. Whereas Nice Guys need to steal the limelight, Good Men are happy giving it away. They do not feel less for listening more often than talking. Good Men rarely compensate and are in tune with their insecurities. They refuse to be diminished by them - perhaps even are empowered despite them - magnifying their presence in simple ways. They are comfortable in their own skin and smile as they leave their comfort zone. Good Men can take a joke and dish it back with class and not make it at the expense of another.

Good Men love to see their people empowered. They do not accentuate themselves among the weak. Instead, they delight in offering time to those willing to better themselves and know that legacy is woven in the small gestures of paying it forward. They celebrate the growth of others, big and small.

They inspire realistically and do not bother with fanfare because they know great work is tedious, tiresome, yet significant. Good Men do not need to exaggerate or inflate reality because they have found a way to romanticize real life despite all the difficulties it throws at them. Good Men are not victims; they are anti-fragile victors who draw every shred of triumph from each season of turmoil.

Good Men live in a harmonious world. They keep themselves dangerous yet only resort to aggression out of absolute necessity. Children learn to communicate and learn their limits through rough-and-tumble play. Good men evolve to an appropriate capacity for aggression and violence yet lead with gentle composure.

Good Men embody the rising tide that raises all ships. Good Men remain wildly underestimated and even more widely underutilized in this crazy world that threatens to turn their focus to temporary highs. Yet good Men will rise to the occasion and sacrifice themselves to unfavourable odds on our behalf.

Nice Guys are inspired by feelings as they arise.

Good Men are consistently inching toward their envisioned life despite their feelings.

Nice Guys want their experience validated.

Good men want to share their experiences.

Nice Guys are slaves to their sexual drives.

Good Men are in control of their libido.

Nice Guys are easily influenced.

Good Men are influential.

Good Men are the unsung heroes whose stories sing of freedom and hope. Sadly, their example is rarely written in history, yet it remains woven into the backbone of their loved ones who carry on.

The memories we sometimes call 'good ole days' are unknowingly shadowed under the safety of Good Men. Most of all, Good Men want you to want all these things from them. They want to be held in high regard so they may be fully utilized. The hardest thing about being a Good Man is consistently maintaining the reasons to be all of these things in a world that would have this power belittled.

Let your love – as a friend or companion - be why a Good Man stands his ground. They aren't indestructible, but a little love goes farther than you think. They only require a bit of appreciation to be kept on the worthy path. At the heart of it all, Good Men do not dominate the weak. They empower them.

The Wickedness that Good Men Are Up Against

I'm pissed off that good men wage war with dignity against those who have none. The injustice seems so rich as good men stay in their lane of integrity as those that muddy our society wage psychological warfare with low blows. Good men are under-utilized until desperation is called upon, and the damage has already been done. Good Men are hard to find as they are rarely found among the pleasures that slowly weave the sorrows of inconsistency, unfaithfulness, immaturity, and addiction.

I believe one of our great failures as a society is how weak and disconnected this overabundance has made us. The excess of pleasures and safety nets allows so many to lean into comforts so heavily that they lose ambitions and goals entirely. Sadness can now be medicated rather than meditated on, and the pain can be a driving force for change that it was always meant to be.

Overabundance has created a vast space for people who add no value to be spiteful of their livelihood while they lack passion and purpose. The will that finds a way is often found in desperation. But desperation used to be a time of radical action. Now, it is a space of self-destruction. We all act like we can't see it coming, with how selfish and tuned-out we can be from each other's true well-being.

In a world that has raised us up in conformity and social status ladders, men are resented and slapped on the wrist for not having their lives and stability planned out. Without stillness, our intuition for our own highest good is drowned out by the mass psychosis of societal expectations. No, I do not speak of a planned mass psychosis but of a mere inability to sit in stillness in a loud world that loves to tell you who you are.

Our society seems to belittle men without direction but isn't nurturing any true self-discovery options to help align their gifts to the world. So, men funnel themselves into jobs that only sustain them but lack inspiration. The resentment of missing out on their potential is easily filled with partying and pleasure-seeking rather than inspiring the blank space where genius and ingenuity are born. It's almost sickening how quickly men step up to accomplish outlandish feats when they are properly loved. They would joyfully crawl over broken glass for anything that inspires them deeply enough. As love is a call to our highest potential, you may suddenly notice how rare that feeling must be in the world of men.

The lack of proper masculine examples has left a world of wounded men who were never given grace and project that pain forward. This then leaves wounded women who become men-haters—so deeply so that many wounded women have lost faith in the possibility of Good Men entirely. Good Men are not only up against raising the bar and inspiring weak men but also soften the traumas left behind in good women. This world truly tests those of generosity and kindness when insecurity and desperation are rampant.

Good Men are the warriors who are in the gardens. They balance the strain of justifying their existence by being valuable and finding people and partners who truly value them. Our best effort is always growing, yet they stumble from time to time. They simply wish to be given the benefit of the doubt and the grace of the long game. They are not done until they are buried. Good men's potential is like the bamboo tree that grows beneath the surface for five years before breaking through and growing ninety feet in five weeks.

Good Men are visionaries who move towards a life yet unseen. They are constantly discredited as dreamers while being the way-makers for the future. The irony is in confidence being quiet, truth never needing to defend itself, and humility never needing to be sung from the rooftops.

Yes, things of value seem to be made scarce by the rule of nature. This does not mean they do not exist; only their value is made rare by the sheer character demanded of them. Their magic is made in the minutia, as Good Men look nothing special, but their spirit moves in such a way that sustains this bizarre world we live in.

Despite it all, Good Men will rise in each era of our fall and bear the weight of rebuilding. It is woven into our souls as our endless ancestors held on to that fragment of faith that our children will do better than we did. This whole story is worth enduring to see such things unfold and move forward. In that alone, we are made as enough, no matter our magnitude. If we raised the wellbeing of anything and anybody of our time, it was our great honour to be of service and spite the gradual promise of atrophy.

That intelligence of calculated anger is what you see in people who rise to the occasion. Those who walk into murky waters to retrieve the lost. Those who have the audacity to stand between evil and the innocent. Those who run into burning buildings. Those who know there are people we disagree with but fight on everybody's behalf for the greater good so we have a safe place to continue figuring it out as generations unfold. Good Men will defy both mankind and nature if it means preserving the things they love. So, diminishing their sense of love and connectedness may be the greatest chink in our armour as a nation.

Despite all their reasons to be bitter and leave the fight to another, Good Men will lay themselves down for anything that gives their life purpose. In a world where men are not born with value and are desperate to earn it, mere appreciation will bring life to the savage servant inside of them. They ask very little yet are prepared to sacrifice all they can for the worthiest cause.

It's no surprise men aren't willing to crawl through mud and die in foxholes on behalf of the whole anymore when digital girlfriends are pleasuring the most useless of them at any whim. The loss of love and belonging has detached them from our foundation of serving one another and society. True love and belonging refuse to allow them to remain pathetic and selfish.

Loving one another may not be as easy as all the pleasures that vie for our attention. Alternatively, society crumbles in the absence of that soulful and savage servitude embedded in them. They yearn to be of service. If nothing and nobody is worthwhile to serve, they meet the ultimate overabundant failure of pleasuring their lonely selves into disease, discontent, and death.

A voluntary willingness to take on responsibility might soon be the only thing that staves off their unbecoming. If they do not do it preventatively, then they will be found weeping in the aftermath of loneliness's fullest manifestation to rampant addictions, self-destruction and suicides.

I'm sorry this is not a feel-good read. But watching people fall out and fall apart in the most overabundant and connected era in history is a cosmic 'whoopsies', to say the least.

I reiterate: Love will save us all. All we ever had was each other. And when the world falls apart, we – the savage servants - will return to one another to put it back together. Our love, our savage servitude, can be the rising tide that sends drifting ships back home to wholeness. Love in service to humanity may sometimes be thankless, but knowing the quality of mankind is preserved through the example is a precious gift.

May the momentum of love's servitude ripple through us in ways our children's children will feel.

Chapter 21

The Sharpest Definition

Our fears are the sharpest definition of who we are. What other metric is more appropriate to weigh us than what stops otherwise pure, unbridled potential?

I've concluded that my two greatest fears are developing dementia/Alzheimer's and the possibility of not becoming a biological father. I will explain how those fears became the best - and perhaps the core - reasons my life has unfolded as it has.

To Love a Memory

What could healthy fear and anger about the possibility of dementia and Alzheimer's mean? If those diagnoses are the gradual decay of memory, cognitive function and physical ability, it means I value the gathering of memories, the growth of my intellect, and my physical ability to enjoy life. If one of the main causes of these sufferings is depression, it means I now am obsessed with everything that spites what creates depressive sensations and habits in my life. The antidote to this is literally the call to adventure. If it *was* to happen, I would want my loved ones to be able to remind me that we really drained the marrow out of life.

I make peace with the real possibility that I have no control over such a fate. Although, if I know the causes, I have a clear-cut task to fend off these preconditions with everything I have. If all that means is that I get extremely intentional with the depth in which I love my life, maximize my health, and spite the decay of my memory by leaving behind things worth remembering, I will happily wage that war every day of my life. I can't wait for celebrations; I have to find the celebration in every fibre of my experience. If all I must do is smite my bitch-ass ego with every act of selflessness, hop on random buses and chuckle in the face of fear, then I've served my soul well.

When writing 'An Arsenal of Gratitude,' I studied many different practices in varied religions and tried many ritualistic habits. I enraptured myself in the stories of people who had every right to believe the world was a sick, unforgiving monster but chose to love their experience and draw the best of it. Cancers, amputations, losing loved ones in freak accidents, violent and war-torn upbringings... the list goes on. Where the most unhinged rage could be justified, gratitude was the almighty common thread that transformed unfathomable suffering into survival guides of reasons we should see this crazy life through. Lo and behold, I started that gratitude journal.

Seven years later, I have over 10,000 individual appreciation points, growth, and celebration. In spite of that fear of losing my memory and capabilities, I am creating the most honest, pure account of my life that I can possibly comprehend. If fear is the sharpest definition of what stops us, then our gratitude is the sharpest definition of what keeps us moving on. I know all too well that it's easy to lose gratitude, but giving up on it seems like the most surefire path to letting the worst of the world have its way with us.

Without the diligent practice of gratitude, it's the bodily equivalent of never physically working out in our lives. We won't die, but we sure as hell won't feel very capable or healthy. Practicing gratitude is the closest thing I believe we have to a spiritual workout. When we and others need a lifeline, we've done enough of our own work to help others find their own reasons to carry on. In turn, they will have everything they need to pay that kindness forward.

The Price of Cowardice

As for the possibility of not being a father, that complexity is a bit different. The fear of not being a father has so many facets for me. It has nothing to do with rushing to get there but the deep desire for a quality that must pre-emptively be nurtured. Few, if anybody, becomes a good father by accident. It is a radical servitude to a family unit. Servitude not only to your lover but to yourself and children all at once. To choose somebody to be an earthly God to a half mini-us together and set the stage for existence for them. We would witness the wonder of everything for the first time all over again through a new, beautifully collaborated essence of ourselves.

I have fallen short countless times while in the midst of what sure seemed like somebody I would fight my forever battles with. I've even walked out of the relationships and opportunities I prayed to be in out of self-pity, shame, doubt, and a pure sense of inadequacy. Those choices and the consequences were so foul to my spirit and those in the crossfire of my self-claimed inadequacy. *All* while those people actively rooted for me.

On top of that, I found my darkest days thanks to proving my fear correct. Perhaps not all people reconcile the same, but I spent the next two years just getting back to a rock-solid state in all emotions that I respect myself. I was never cruel or malicious, but my cowardice manifested the most obvious obstacles between who I was and who I was becoming. My own fear of not having yet 'arrived' to a maximally capable self had me self-sabotaging perfectly good things in front of me. As if anybody *ever* is at that point. But here we all are despite exactly that sort of imperfection from our parents, aren't we?

All I could see was the seemingly impossible gap between myself and my self-expectation. My fear of not *yet* being that man belittled my current moment, and I forbade my own joy. I became the bad thing that could happen. I was suffering from my own intelligence.

The visionary quality I love about myself had a completely broken concept of what it should be and how I could make it so. The gap, or my lack of action to make it so, was becoming proof that my vision and its lack of fruition was my own fault.

The solution became finding every conceivable way to embody my future as a great dad in this present moment. If I envisioned my highest being as a great dad (In my opinion), I'd have to be the most emotionally intelligent and patient man to weather the battles with the woman of my dreams. She's going to be a firecracker, so I better have my shit together to be able to tame and worship that magnificence with the proper balance.

I'd have to be the most disciplined person I know to live out the example I would love for my children. I must have as little space between what I say and how I act as possible. I would have to be an absolute physical specimen, so when my future son inevitably has the "My dad could beat up your dad" argument, I want him to be right 100% of the time.

That's *mostly* a tasteful joke, but I want to prove to my family all the wonderful things that can be accomplished when humans try to maximize their unique potential. I would have to dedicate myself to my best understanding of the healthiest lifestyle so I can celebrate the unfolding of my own generations before me.

I would strive to be the most reliable friend on the planet. I would regularly check in on friends and be ok with often being the initiator to normalize appreciation for no reason but the sake of itself. I would end my hesitation of receiving gifts and be the greatest gift-giver despite the ways I have been hardened by having my kindness taken advantage of. I want my enthusiasm to be intoxicating and overflow into their well-being. I would have to frequently ask for them to help audit my life so I'm not bullshitting any of my own ambitions and have every uncomfortable conversation possible. I want the safety of my space to be where others consider it to be their home as well.

I would have to revive my child-like curiosity to teach my children how to explore and love the world. I would have to constantly sharpen my senses and continue learning so my children's perspective can witness everyday magic. I would have to humanize suffering and humble myself to have bad days in front of my kids so they don't feel separate from others in their shortcomings. I would have to admit I don't know what's next most of the time, but I will always be in tune with what keeps my soul on fire. I would have to find the silver lining in every tragedy to draw beauty from hardships.

I would have to make peace with my money-fears, as I may not be entirely financially secure when bringing a child into the world. I would dishonour every parent who made thin ends meet without their children ever knowing. I must not deny my children's challenges. If anything, I would be inclined to propel them towards things that seem stacked against their odds. I would have to live on my edge to be a living example of meaningful risks as a way to an abundant life.

I would have to be a God-fearing man who never plays as if I am immune to the consequences of my actions. I would have to be radically accountable and be the proper example and cautionary tale for my mishaps. This, aligned with my abstaining from pornography, is a radical dedication to funnelling all my life's energy in the most meaningful directions I can give it. How could I possibly be all-in with the love of my life if I'm worshipping any other body than hers?

I can practice every single one of those characteristics today. I believe I am in the midst of manifesting all of that character and beginning to reap the rewards of the vast richness in my relationships, home life, adventures, and faith in the future.

Between the push of outworking my fear and the pull of a vision for a very specific future, I have a maximally potent drive to bring this to fruition. Leaving behind everything that doesn't fit this golden future of mine is the most direct path to making space for it. In everything that broke my heart, I discovered exactly what is and isn't for my highest being. For that alone, heartbreak has become an essential gift for my becoming.

Revelation

Returning to that chapter on people being 'Out of My League,' we have a quick example of shifting self-worth. If something or somebody so mesmerizing and desirable crosses your orbit and your entire being wants to do *something* about it and you do nothing, that is a definition of your self-value. If it is something that scares the hell out of you and you act *despite* your fear, you have redefined who you are in one single act. That is *no* joke. In theory, if you can tackle just one monumental task against your insecurity, then by default, everything comparatively less intimidating is within your reach, right?

I recognized how the different emotional states of my being were bargaining with each other. It's a strange thing to admit that I've spent so long arguing with my own free will and well-being that I can sense a bullshitter from a mile away. I have well-versed myself in the language of self-deceit. Our ability to outsmart our higher judgment proves what primitive beasts of desire we truly are. There is no lacking dignity in being *unaware* of the consequences of curiosity, but then returning to something that has *proven* to be against our well-being says a lot about our human condition. We have embedded programming so deep of sensory hunger that we betray our own greatest potential *willingly* to experience things we knowingly hate ourselves for after.

If there was logic to be had in that bargaining with ourselves, then the stern 'you know better' should suffice. The problem is, we *know* that. Yet we still gnaw at the universal consequences of our actions repeatedly until we are sick of the person in the mirror and are surprised by how we got there. This battle between the self and our primitive nature is the most significant battle of our entire life. That idea of a higher self is a patient anomaly that is begging to grow and guide a fantastic, adventurous life.

Whereas, that primitive nature is the thousands - perhaps millions - of years of programming embedded into our genetics. We are quite literally arguing with our ancestors. Who else could these voices in our head be? Who is the plaintiff, the defendant, the jury and the judge in our mind? Why do they never explicitly separate themselves for our sanity's sake? And for all that matter, who is the one listening?

The brain is the only thing in the universe that named itself. How has the thing that named itself become so powerful as to change the world yet crumbled under its own potential?

What does this have to do with fear and defining ourselves? I discovered that I always lose the argument against my greater good if I give the lesser voice long enough. Emotion's craving to be consoled at the moment is rarely—if ever—aligned with my ultimate goal. There are parts of us that we must console and others we must overpower. You must win some battles before the conflict knocks on your door. This is where I share how to ethically invalidate your momentary desires and temptations.

Bluntly: Fuck your feelings. You have a goal. Your feelings don't care about your goal. But your highest calling does.

If you want to quit or start a new habit, you must make a predetermined promise that makes all future decisions when sticking to your promises and plans. Your true test is not when the plan makes sense but when sticking to your promises is inconvenient.

The Sharpest Definition

When loneliness knocks, you've already decided not to text your exes or watch porn. When offered a drink or smoke at a party, you've already emotionally practiced, 'No, thank you' with a smile. You either eliminate environments altogether or have supports engrained to make bad habits inconvenient or good habits difficult to avoid.

I've lost most battles with myself *well* before the actual event that I consider a failure of a self-promise. There was a bargaining well before. I abso-friggin-lutely did *not* stumble into my stupidly. I slowly and deliberately tiptoed every step towards it.

We do not have tendencies or habits; we have *choices*. Just like momentum, the micro-gestures are subtle and sinister steps to making soft 'whoopsies' back into our bullshit. When you enter a world of radical freedom, you must own every fibre of your actions. Otherwise, you submit to being a half-conscious animal that surrenders to primal urges. An animal that is only as reliable as your threshold of convenience. An animal that others will learn to fear and avoid any time anything is stressful enough for you.

I want to live in a world where we practice our spirits to be truly free against all odds and urges.

A promise is the epitome of a choice that declares 'no matter what…' it can be done. That means if that word can even exist and we can use it, then we also believe we have the power to transcend all difficulties attached to that claim. These words only hold as much weight as we give them. Otherwise, promises are diminished to sweet verbal foreplay that only breaks your and everybody else's hearts.

Here is my lesson: I know the sound of my highest being by the lack of begging for compromise. I cannot maintain self-respect and my claim to free will if I doubt that I can outsmart the sorrowful temptations that tomorrow's struggle may bring. In this alone, I limit the sorrow across my entire lifetime by denying the validity of sorrow's pleas.

Every attempt to escape reality in a drunk, a high, or a habit stemmed from a sober thought. We walk ourselves right into those blind states of being every single time. One cannot purify one's lifestyle without taking radical ownership of their actions. Alternatively, the sheer hopelessness of surrendering to not being in control would have already taken hold of the entire human race. The smallest shred of free will in our consciousness is the indomitable seed of a sequoia tree if we only discover how to nurture it properly.

I'm pissed off that we don't all agree that our intelligence is a love note from the universe. Our free will could be celebrated every day if we just understood that we could redesign our relationships to fear. If we can see that, we can rewrite the narrative of how we cower from self-inflicted distress. That complete delusion of validating anxiety and fear convinces us that we can predict the future, but only in a manner that confirms how small we are as the verdict. Every new thriving act should be written in our journal as the unfathomable magnificence of our free will.

I'm pissed off that we suffer our own magnificence. I'm pissed off people are so committed to their distress that the enthusiasm of others is received as immaturity or naivety. We did not come so far into existence to be our own worst enemy. Understanding our nature to manifest ourselves as our worst enemy should be as essential as learning the alphabet. If we can, at the very least, understand ourselves enough to know who we *don't* want to be, then the human experience can become the playground it was meant to be for who we choose to become.

It seems like a small ask, though I must re-iterate: The battle against ourselves is and will continue to be the greatest battle in our lifetime. If we can conquer ourselves, we can conquer all else. As each of us succeeds, we stiffen the spines of others as proof that we are always meant to walk tall.

CHAPTER 22

This Mountain is Mine

*T*his mountain has been assigned to you to show others that it can be moved.

The story you tell yourself is truly the heart of it all. I managed to wrap this weight of childhood cancer survivor's guilt up into a spiritual gift and called it a mission for gratitude and service to mankind. Even when we 12-year-old kids gathered in pure shock as our common friend, Davis, relapsed and lost his battle against the same Leukemia I had, we decided the only appropriate response was to live more bravely. We take it upon ourselves to make up for the life he did not get to grow up into and live alongside us.

We decided to live out the anthem: *There is Bravery in This World.*

Choosing to live a wholehearted, courageous life is also a trauma response. Perhaps not a trauma *reaction*, but certainly a trauma *response*.

These sorrows are serendipities in the making if I calibrate my spiritual compass that way. If something is going to haunt me, you best believe I will use that story to harvest miracles. This valley I was born into, and the mountains of misery are where I find my own self-mastery. I receive these seemingly insurmountable woes before me like a dare from God to turn it into another verse for this ultimate song. This is the anthem that the next generation will grow up on and be nourished by.

There is Bravery in This World.

My disposition towards my life is more valuable than my current position. If it were not for these pains, pleasures would not be so sweet.

How do you make somebody strong? You probably wouldn't give them unlimited comfort and ease. You'd probably give them meaningful challenges that border limitations. It would probably involve incredible failure, trial and error, curiosity, flexibility and dedication to accomplish genuine fortitude.

So, what do we gain from unique difficulty? Unique insight and unique experience. We get to experience our abnormal reaction to abnormal situations. We may be so lifted from our frame of understanding that we are forced to form solutions to problems nobody would wish upon another. But the tragedies life offers do not discriminate.

So, we become unified through devastation. We lend courage, hope, humility and raw connection in times of difficulty and rebuilding. But we cannot do any of that if we are committed to our bullshit attempt at acting invincible, flawless and always in control.

I claim every experience that has been bestowed upon me as an opportunity to amplify the ultimate song of humanity. These traumas, these addictions, these fears, these heartbreaks. These mistakes, these ambitions, these intuitions, these desires.

This mountain is mine.

All the bullshit I've lied about. The ways that I've lacked integrity and instilled my own lack of peace. The way that I've fed into my own hopelessness and despaired. The ways that I've lost touch with gratitude and bought into the possibility my efforts are meaningless.

This mountain is mine.

These relationships I will have to end and dreams that I will have to let die so something greater can take its place. This fumbling around in the dark for love and experimenting with my talents to maximize my gifts to the world. These damn fears that cling to my heels every step of new meaningful experience as I dance on the edge of possibility.

This. Mountain. Is. Mine.

The World Can Hear Your Heartbeat

You are here to be devastated. You are here to have your heart out. You are here to be swallowed up. You will come from the womb of a woman, and you will end in the womb of the earth. You owe creation a death. You owe humanity a story-worthy life. Stop avoiding the question: What do you want to do with this one terrifying, unpredictable, and beautifully brief life?

Remember this: You underestimate yourself in direction proportion to how much you believe in your insecurities. The injustice you feel in hearing that is the fuel you need to spite those insecurities. You build momentum in self-defeat or self-mastery. You decide.

The quality of life is not measured in success or failure. It is measured in love over fear. It doesn't have to be perfect; it just has to be done. It has to be lived. Love doesn't fail; it redirects. Love is not wins over losses; it is courage over cowardice.

Returning back to those six kinds of courage is how we become multi-dimensionally jacked. We offer ourselves to one another through our stories. We unfold before one another and weave into each other's lives and make it more than before. If you understand the magnitude of the impact that we could have on one another, your life and sense of responsibility will forever change. You are in a league of one and only in competition with your own small-mindedness. As you prioritize conquering yourself, you can shift to collaborating with the collective instead of competing against it.

I understand fully well I am yet to be shaken to the core in ways I cannot comprehend. Whether I face cancer again or whether it is my loved ones. Whether war comes to our doorstep. Whether I go out in a freak accident or hit my head and lose all my memories. One thing I have no shadow of a doubt about: Gratitude is how we wage war on mediocrity and regret.

After seven years and over ten thousand notes of gratitude, it has unknowingly created a spiritual compass. Just five minutes every night to take account of the blessings, the beauty I saw in others, how I reacted to difficulty, how I can show up differently and how profoundly life changes in a moment. So much magic is hiding in the world right before us. We could be so profoundly enriched by what we write about our own life every night when we realize we are the master-crafter of this crazy journey. Let the audacity fly, and give yourself a story worth telling! It is unreasonable to create any extraordinary habit and not eventually accomplish extraordinary results.

Along that journey, feel no guilt when you sit under a tree and enjoy the shade for the sake of itself. Breathe deeply. There is no shame in slowing down long enough to remember everything you really have in front of you. We are all feeling around in the dark to find one another.

Fumbling forward in a day can fracture into a future of beauty that could never have been comprehended until we are standing there. But the only way to see ten feet farther through the fog is to walk ten feet further. The only thing we bargain with is the consequences of how we live truly free.

All life aspires to what music does. Each note is no greater or lesser than another. The sake of itself is enough; every note is part of a greater whole. All expression is an extension of the bigger story. Every off-beat note may be a cringe-worthy feeling, but that only shows how *deeply* and *instinctively* we desire harmony. You cannot skip to the good parts or the end. To skip any part would be a great disservice to the art of the entire song. You can't rip chapters from a book and say you know its depth. The same goes for us.

Did you know that people's heartbeats will synchronize if they are close together for long enough? We will mimic our physiological and emotional states through emotional connection, physical proximity, shared activities, and empathy. That means our magnificence could literally become contagious. But so can our anxiety and fearfulness. Which would you rather share and instill in others?

The Most Courageous Day of Your Life

Do you need more theory? Or do you need dirt on your hands?

Eventually, you have far more than you need to start because the people you're studying started with less. That's why you are consuming their content. A professional is anybody who is two steps ahead of you. So, any fool who at least started and has gotten sweat equity is already a professional compared to those too scared to start. Being somebody who always studies and never actualizes on their craft has shifted from studying into mental masturbation.

When you quit playing with yourself, you can begin to go play with the world. It's the same as studying conversation tactics to get a date. There is no high quite like going into the wild and saying hello. Every time fear wins, it is strengthened. It only takes one courageous effort to take that power back.

What would the most courageous day of your life look like? If you listen long enough, your soul will know what it wants. The fact that you can *imagine* being more courageous proves you have untapped potential.

If you're going to convince yourself that your fantasies are impossible, then get smaller fantasies. Quit insulting your intelligence and potential by taunting yourself with ideals you refuse to fight for. *All you need is an empowering story of what it is, how it ought to be, and a realistic action plan for how you can make it so.*

If this book serves its purpose, you will stop rejecting yourself. You will fuck around and find out. You will shed limiting beliefs and challenge them at every corner. You will accept criticism with gratitude. You will become anti-fragile, stronger with every tribulation.

You will unapologetically express your playful side. You will be relentlessly curious. You will be an epic cheerleader for others and not let their spirit wane. You will capture yourself in the middle of laughter and adventure and soak in the appreciation of the world and those you share it with.

You will be your own unapologetic sort of weird and wonderful. You will harvest your own miracles and serendipities from the adventures and talents that beckon to you. You will pay it forward with whatever enthusiasm and kindness you have to leave this strange home of ours better than you found it. You will sow all the love you can muster into the world to see how it blooms and bounces back for you.

It's Go Time

I am endlessly grateful that of all things to do on earth, you chose to wage war on fear. I hope you are enriched through my testimony and get absolutely audacious with your experience of love for this life. Let me offer you these final words to claim for yourself:

May it be that when I speak, it improves upon silence.

May it be that when I move, it improves upon stillness.

May I make peace with all that is outside of my control. May I be disciplined enough to move with massive action yet hold my practice to be captivated by the little things.

May I walk the fine line that both the universe and I are playing our finest ends to bring forth the highest outcome.

May my rage be calculated so evil will shiver in my wake while my loved ones sleep easy. May I be meaner than evil.

May my guilt course-correct my spirit appropriately and lead to greater harmony. May my grief amplify how deeply I love each moment. May my sorrow be crafted into survival guides.

May I leave this world better than I found it. May my love linger and drown out the bitterness and resentments of the world. May my stumbling forward inspire the magnificence of others.

May all our hearts beat like music and remind one another that there is bravery in this world.

About the Author

Remmy is a river-crossing, mountain-climbing, horseback-riding, story-crafting, cancer-surviving man of faith and action. He is dedicated to magnifying a world of gratitude, courage, and wholeheartedness in humanity at every turn. In honour of his upbringing with the Kids Cancer Care Foundation of Alberta, 10% of all book proceeds are donated in hopes of passing on the opportunity to the next generation of young survivors.

Thank You + Connect

You could be doing anything else on earth, yet you are here. I am grateful for your time, and I hope you feel empowered moving forward in this one life.

If you'd like to connect, collaborate or celebrate something, feel free to reach out to <u>remmystourac@hotmail.com</u>

For more content, find me on Instagram, Facebook, and Tiktok @RemmyStourac.

If you enjoyed the book, please consider leaving a review. Even a line or two would be incredibly helpful!

Notes

---

[i] National Institute of Mental Health. n.d. "Suicide." National Institute of Mental Health. Accessed February 10, 2025. https://www.nimh.nih.gov/health/statistics/suicide.

[ii] National Center for Health Statistics, "Suicide Mortality in the United States, 1999–2019," *Centers for Disease Control and Prevention*, accessed February 10, 2025, https://www.cdc.gov/nchs/products/databriefs/db377.htm.

[iii] John A. Cramer, "The COVID-19 Pandemic and Suicide: A Call to Action," *Psychological Trauma: Theory, Research, Practice, and Policy* 12, no. S1 (2020): S233–S235, https://www.ncbi.nlm.nih.gov/pmc/articles/PMC7437849/.

[iv] The Holy Bible, 1 Corinthians 14:33 (KJV).

[v] Matam, Pages. "Piñata." In The Heart of a Comet. Write Bloody Publishing, 2014. Line 12.

[vi] The Holy Bible, 1 Peter 5:8 (NIV).

www.ingramcontent.com/pod-product-compliance
Lightning Source LLC
Chambersburg PA
CBHW020419010526
44118CB00010B/319